IMAGES
of America

COTATI

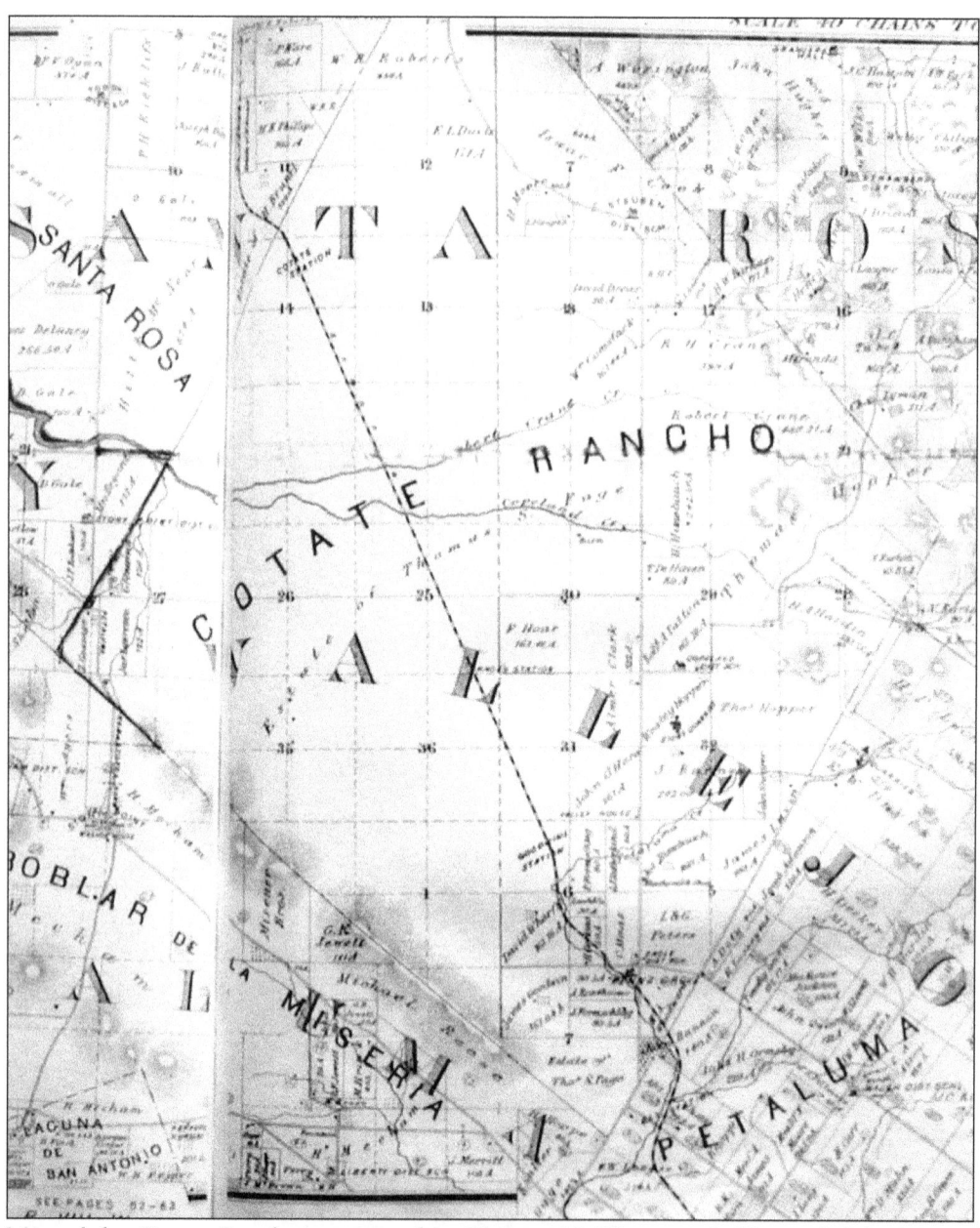

Map of the Cotate Rancho as pictured in Thomas H. Thompson's *Historical Atlas Map of Sonoma County, California*, 1877. The map shows portions of the large diamond-shaped land grant that had been deeded to new settlers, many of them squatters who homesteaded while the land titles were being decided. After receiving his patent in 1857, Dr. Thomas Stokes Page sold land to many of those settlers. (Courtesy Sonoma County Library.)

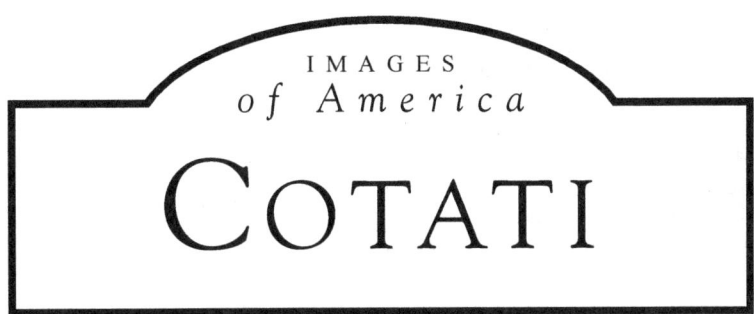

IMAGES
of America
COTATI

Prudence and Lloyd Draper

ARCADIA
PUBLISHING

Published by Arcadia Publishing
Charleston, South Carolina

Library of Congress Catalog Card Number: 2004100108

For all general information contact Arcadia Publishing at:
Telephone 843-853-2070
Fax 843-853-0044
E-mail sales@arcadiapublishing.com
For customer service and orders:
Toll-Free 1-888-313-2665

Visit us on the Internet at www.arcadiapublishing.com

Several different versions of the Cotati City Limits sign have been used over the years since Cotati became a city in 1963. This one was proposed by Thomas Byrne in 1979 and has influenced designs ever since.

CONTENTS

Acknowledgments   6

Introduction   7

1.   A Fertile Land Draws Settlers   9

2.   One Huge Ranch Becomes Many Small Ones   25

3.   A Community Develops   37

4.   The Auto Years   53

5.   Proud to Be the "Hub of Sonoma County"   71

6.   A New College, A New City, A New Age   93

7.   Cotati Encounters the Counter Culture   109

8.   An Interesting, if Reluctant, Blend   123

ACKNOWLEDGMENTS

The authors knew that little had been published about Cotati in the past, but didn't realize, when they embarked on producing this book, that it would excite so many people and turn out to be the community effort that it has become. Sincere thanks go to the many, many friends, neighbors, city officials, relatives, and new acquaintances who encouraged us in this effort, loaned us their cherished family photos, consented to our dismantling their scrapbooks, and helped us with identifications.

Special thanks go to Simone Wilson, Creighton Bell, Jerry Pagnusat and Keith Eggel, who helped us weather the computer storms that threatened to sink the project. Thanks, too, to our editor, Hannah Clayborn, who offered advice and assistance as we made our way through the maze of details. The list of all who helped would go on and on, but some are the following: John Allred, Sara Anna, George and Teresa Arthur, Anna Marie Avanzino, Margaret and Charlie Baranzini, Gene Benedetti, Artie Bourboulis, Lena Braden, Patty Brott, Kathy Brisbine, Lindy Brown, Flo Casarotti, Frank Castelli, John and Jacquie DelOsso, Dee Delevois, Dennis Dorch, Jennie Falletti, Bob Foreman, John Gaines, Bert Glick, Harold Griffith, Frank Hayhurst, Tony Hoskins, John Hughes, Gary Isha Isringhaus, Lillian Jasperson, Evelyn Johnstone, Bill and Lucy Kortum, Gaye LeBaron, Lew Levinson, Millie Libarle, Mary Nell McCann, Eleanor Miller, Jerry Miller, Lisa Moore, John Muller, Christine Myers, Bob and Mabel Nelson, Kiyo Okazaki, Paul Otani, John Page, George Parrish, B.B. Paulekas, Anita and Donald Ray, Dayle Reilly, Marguerite Revard, Mattie and Jack Rudinow, Barney and Evelin Santero, Jud Snyder, Eric Stanley, Donna Stegman, Dave and Elaine Thomas, and Anthony Tusler.

We also thank our family, Bob, Ellen, Robin, and Erin Draper, who patiently bore our distracted schedule and house filled with photos and notes. We especially dedicate this book to Marguerite Hahn and Kay Nylander, whose careful work years ago photographing and documenting Cotati's day-to-day life and preserving it in scrapbooks made this book possible.

INTRODUCTION

Many of the Coast Miwok Indians who had lived in the Cotate Valley for generations disappeared after the first Spanish settlers arrived. White man's diseases and forced labor in the missions and forts took their toll.

No English-speaking settlers attempted to make their homes here until 1826, when John Thomas Reed arrived. Born in Ireland in 1805, he came as a teenager to the New World, and in his travels became acquainted with the San Francisco area. After the Mexican War of Independence he sought land in Sausalito, but learned about the Cotati Valley after talking to Jose Antonio Sanchez, an early Spanish settler. Reed traveled to the Sonoma Mission, then over the mountains to the Cotati area, built a cabin, and planted wheat. Before he could harvest his first crop, he was burnt out by Indians, probably as they carried out their annual practice of burning grasslands to harvest small rodents and snakes to augment their diet. Discouraged, Reed went to Marin where he built a successful mill and became a prominent citizen of Mill Valley.

Reed died young, apparently without ever having his photograph taken. But accounts by people who knew him in Marin describe him as "a fine specimen of manhood, notably tall and well-proportioned, with deep blue eyes, good complexion, and crisp blonde hair."

As part of the Mexican government's effort to settle California, the Rancho Cotate land grant was established, occupying a 17,000 acre diamond-shaped area in the center of what became Sonoma County. It was first granted in 1844 to Captain Juan Castenada, who built a house and bought stock, but sold the claim two years later to Thomas O. Larkin. Larkin, the American consul at Monterey, sold it in 1849 to Joseph S. Ruckle, who sold it two months later to Dr. Thomas Page of Valparaiso, Chile.

Dr. Page apparently had been urged by his friend Faxon Atherton to buy land and bring his family to California. Finally, the Rancho Cotate had a permanent owner.

The Page family's ownership continued until 1944, when the final portions of the huge ranch were sold, the last of the Spanish land grants in Sonoma County to be subdivided. The community that began after 1893, when the Page family laid out the town of Cotate, grew quickly. Most of the new settlers were farmers, following the lead of nearby Petaluma, where raising chickens for eggs was already a thriving industry. The town that grew up served those small farmers, offering them general merchandise, livestock feed, and vegetables, while buying up their eggs.

In 1915 the State of California chose what had been Cotati Boulevard as the main highway between Petaluma and Santa Rosa, and the Cotati scene changed. Autos made the difference, and garages, service stations, and restaurants appeared to serve the motoring public.

When a new route west of downtown Cotati was chosen for the 101 freeway in 1955, Cotati changed again. The poultry business became unprofitable for small family farms, major traffic bypassed downtown Cotati, and a family-oriented community for commuters began to evolve. The town had organized to provide water and sewer service, had streetlights, and the active chamber of commerce was fiercely proud of the little community and its distinctive six-sided plaza, advertising itself as the "Hub of Sonoma County."

Further radical changes came to Cotati with the establishment of Sonoma State College in 1960 and the beginning of development in Rohnert Park on what had been the hay fields of the Page Ranch and later the seed farm of the Waldo Rohnert Company. Rohnert Park, master-planned and built at a fast pace, was an astonishing development for residents of the small farm town. Suddenly the Cotati Volunteer Fire Department had to protect new homes in what had traditionally been farm fields, and the Cotati School District began putting students on double session while building new schools.

When Rohnert Park incorporated as a city, Cotati saw its rural lifestyle threatened, and incorporated itself as a separate city. The two municipalities interlocked on several boundaries, but had drastically differing philosophies—Rohnert Park dedicated to rapid growth and compact development; Cotati retaining its farmer roots, thinking twice about every change.

Students from Sonoma State, soon to become a full four-year state university, loved Cotati. Like college students all over the U.S. in the 1960s and 1970s, they embraced "back to the earth" movements. The unused chicken houses of Cotati ranches made perfect low-rent apartments. The tree-shaded lawn of LaPlaza Park was a wonderful place for dancing, drumming, and meditating with their friends. Music, always important in Cotati, became an even more prominent part of life, with famous bands drawing large audiences to local venues.

Students in 1973 decided their voices should be heard, and rallied supporters to overwhelm three long-time residents in an election for City Council. Ten years of change in the city's philosophy followed, with several recall efforts, resignations of several city councilmen, firing of several city managers, and meetings that went well into the night.

As Sonoma State University changed, reflecting high-tech development in the county, and the hippies matured, so Cotati evolved also. Its location in the center of a fast-growing county at the intersection of highways 101 and 116, convenient for commuters, lured developers, and large neighborhoods of new homes and several small shopping areas were created.

The city today still reflects its varied history: a few small farms remain, usually as hobbies for their owners, often lying close to clusters of apartment dwellers. The city still has a preponderance of independent business owners, but also has a growing number of larger stores. It is still a local live entertainment mecca, with ethnic restaurants, sidewalk cafes, and music festivals.

Cotati's emphasis is on the quality of life, with the older and newer residents still striving to decide just how to define "quality."

One

A FERTILE LAND DRAWS SETTLERS

The name Cotate came from a tribelet of Coast Miwok Indians, the Kota'ti, who had lived in this fertile valley for at least 5,000 years. They were a peaceful people, and there was no shortage of deer, birds, and small animals, which they hunted with bow and arrow, fish in the streams, and berries and bulbs to give them a healthy diet. Acorns, ground into mush with mortar and pestles, were their staff of life. Ceremonies and dances were an important part of their culture, and they decorated themselves with feathers and animal skins as well as tattoos. The legend of a chief named Cotate has been passed down for years, but there is no documentation for his existence.

Coast Miwok Indians built shelters of tree bark or tules, tied in a conical shape with strips of tree bark. A fire in the center kept them warm in winter. Acorns were stored in granaries built in a similar manner. (Courtesy of Pt. Reyes National Seashore.)

The dance house was the most important gathering place in a Coast Miwok village. Here meetings and dances were held to celebrate important events, cure sickness, or pray for a good harvest. The house was excavated and the roof mounded, with the ceiling held up by posts tied into place with vines and covered with mats, brush, leaves, and clay. (Courtesy of Pt. Reyes National Seashore.)

This communal mortar stone, shown by Jack Rudinow, was discovered on a creek bank near Petaluma Hill Road. In this view it is raised from its horizontal position to show the deep holes where Miwok women ground acorns into meal, using stone pestles. It is one of many Miwok artifacts found in the local area. Smaller individual mortars were also common. (Courtesy of Mattie and Jack Rudinow.)

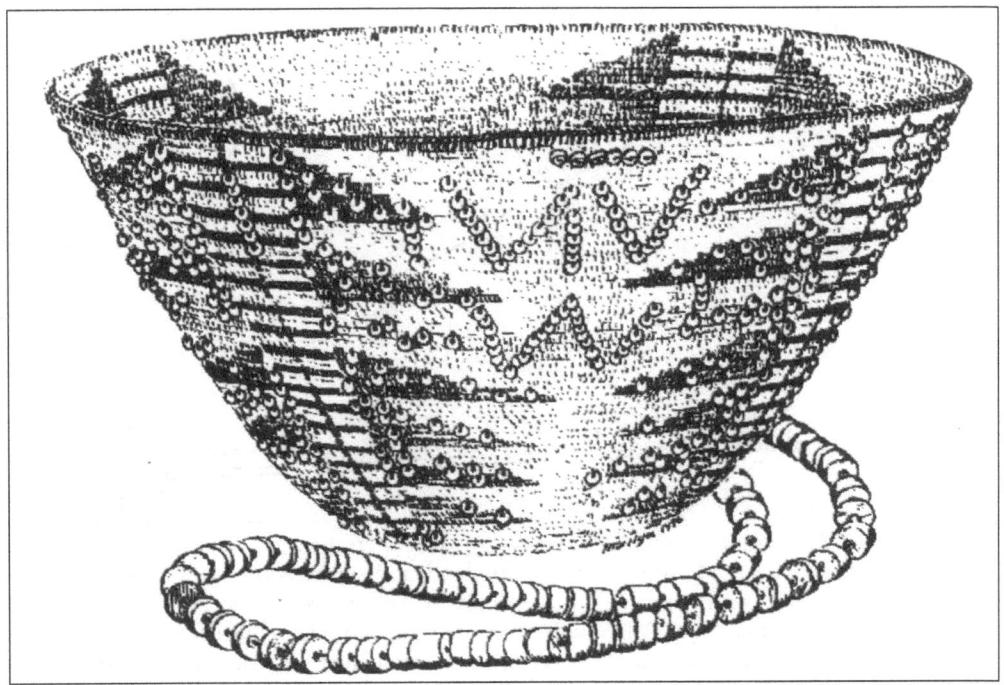

Baskets woven of willow branches, sedge roots, and redbud were used for gathering fruit, vegetables, acorns, and seeds. Acorn mush was cooked in baskets by filling them with water and dropping in hot rocks. Shell beads made of discs of clam shell decorated some baskets and were used as ornamental belts or as money. (Courtesy of Pt. Reyes National Seashore.)

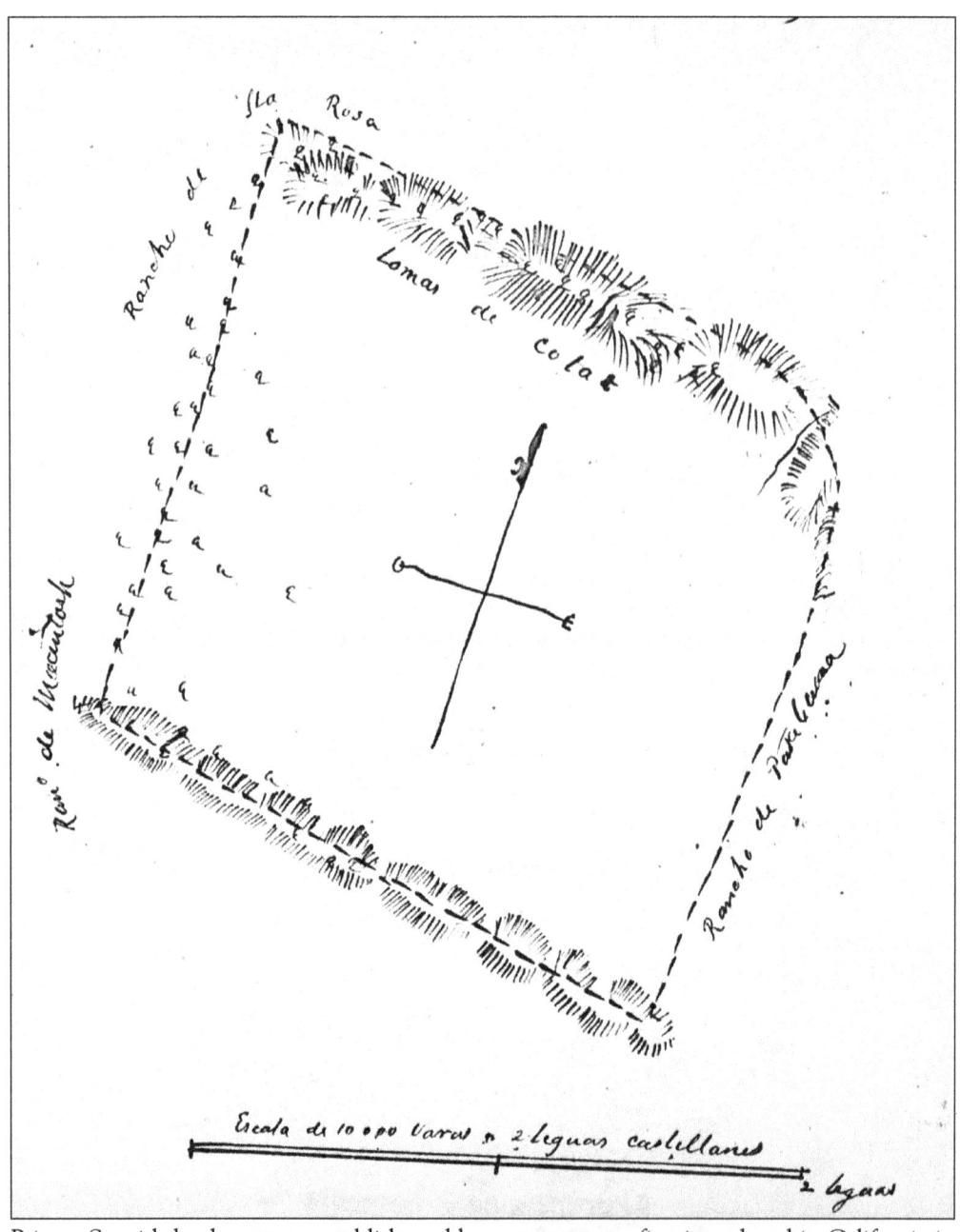

Private Spanish land grants to establish pueblos or towns were first introduced in California in 1774. By 1828, rules for establishing and claiming land grants were adopted. A Mexican citizen could apply for a grant, setting forth location boundaries or approximate size and testifying that it did not overlap another grant. A land survey was carried out under a magistrate with witnesses from neighboring ranchos. The surveyors used a 50-foot rawhide cord tied to stakes that riders thrust into the ground as they rode along, and a diseño (sketch-map) was produced. This was the diseño for the Rancho Cotate, used in proving Dr. Thomas Stokes Page's claim of ownership.

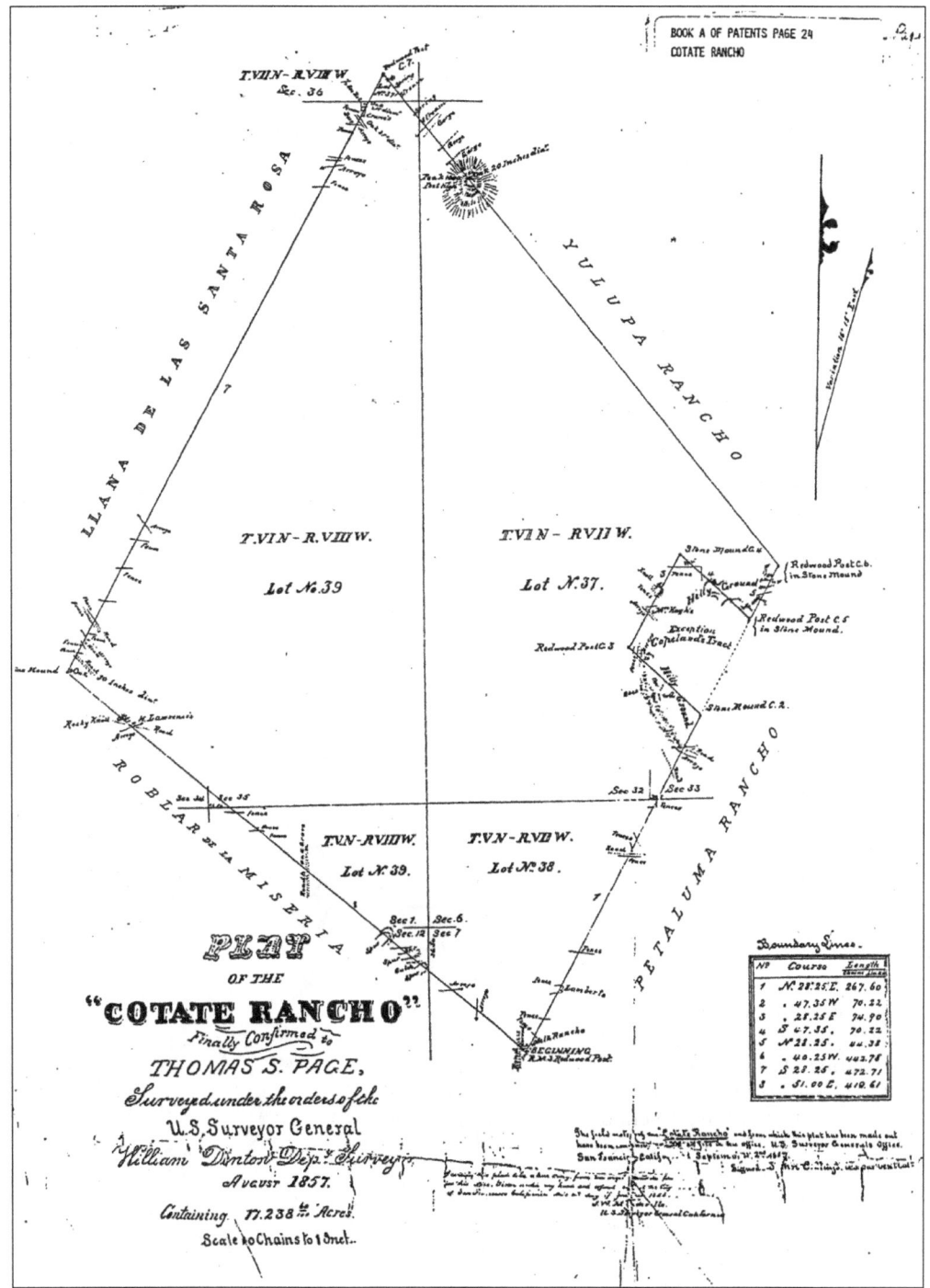

This map was issued when the Page land grant claim was patented in 1857. It had taken Dr. Page five years before the U.S. District Court confirmed his ownership of the 17,238.60-acre land grant.

Dr. Thomas Stokes Page was born in 1815 in Moorestown, New Jersey, and after graduating from the University of Pennsylvania Medical School in 1836, he sailed to Europe. After touring England and France, he sailed to Valparaiso, Chile, where he had decided to start his medical practice. He became one of the most celebrated physicians in the country, and in 1849 purchased the Rancho Cotate land grant. He made at least one trip to Cotate in the 1860s to take a look at his land, which he had purchased sight unseen, and began establishing a stock ranch. He brought most of his large family here in 1869.

Anna Maria Liljevalch, the daughter of Olof Liljevalch of Sweden and Mary Anne Delano of Massachusetts, married Dr. Page in 1841 in Valparaiso. In 1842 the first of their 13 children, Olof, was born. Thereafter came Henry, Charles, Wilfred, Anita, Caroline, twins Arthur and George, George Thomas, Maria Teresa, Lizzie, Manuela, and William Delano. Three of the children, Caroline, Maria Teresa, and the twin George, died in infancy. All the others came with their parents to Cotate except Henry and Olof, who stayed in Valparaiso. Olof, also a physician, took over his father's medical practice.

The home built by Dr. Page for his family topped the hillside above El Rancho Avenue. It had 16 rooms, tall ceilings, high windows, a fireplace in every room, winding staircases, and many stained glass windows. The family lived there only part of the time, for they also owned a home in San Francisco, and Mrs. Page and her daughters preferred urban rather than rural life. Wilfred and his brother William managed the ranch after Dr. Page died in 1872. Pictured here in 1895 are left to right, Wilfred Page, son Roy, Mrs. Wilfred Page, and daughters, Elizabeth and Edith. The house was used as a country home and headquarters for the ranching operation through the 1920s, but fell into disrepair. Badly damaged by fire in the 1930s, it was demolished in the 1940s. (Courtesy of John R. Page.)

This huge six-sided barn was built by Dr. Thomas Page soon after he arrived to begin his ranch. The reason why he chose this hexagonal design for the barn and a large water tank outside are unknown. The barn could store 1,100 tons of baled hay. In later years it was owned by the Sebastopol Meat Co. and used as a feed lot. The barn was demolished in 1962 when the new St. Joseph's Church was built on the site.

Wifred Page (*left*) was the manager of his family's Cotate Rancho. He married Ema Adams and they had seven children. After the ranch was sold, he became a stockbroker in San Francisco. Charles Page (*right*) became an attorney in San Francisco. He married Sally Myers in 1856 and they had three children.

Arthur Page (*left*) and George T. Page (*right*) formed the firm Page Brothers, ship and merchandise brokers, in San Francisco. Arthur married Emelita Ralston and they had two children. George married Georgie Hammond and they had one child.

William Delano Page, (*left*) born in 1867, was an infant when the family came to California. His father's will stipulated that the ranch not be divided until Willie was 25. He assisted on the ranch and later became his brother's partner in their ship brokerage. Anita Page, (*right*) born in 1851, returned to Chile with her brother Henry. She married George Thomas Smith and later Benito Smith and they had one child, Edith.

Manuela Page (*left*) was born in 1863 in Valparaiso. She married Horatio Hellman. Elizabeth "Lizzie" Page (*right*) was born in 1861 in Valparaiso. She married John W. Mailliard in 1888 and they had five children. (All Page family photos from the collection of Robin Skewes-Cox, courtesy of John R. Page.)

Many Indian and Mexican workers were employed in the Cotate Rancho operation. In 1880, perhaps not too long before this photo was taken, a settler reported that he had seen 30 black bears grazing on clover in the Cotate plains. (Courtesy of Petaluma Library and Museum.)

Title to Dr. Page's claim to the Rancho Cotate was clouded in confusion during the Bear Flag Rebellion and Dr. Page was not able to confirm his ownership of the land until 1858. By then, several settlers had laid squatter's claim to his land, and started farms. Later Dr. Page sold these farms to them. Pictured here are farm workers and a threshing machine *c.* 1890.

When Dr. Page died in 1872 he left his 9,668 acres of property to his family. The huge ranch raised hay, barley, and oats, and Wilfred Page was listed in the 1890 Polk Directory as a stock raiser, wool grower, and breeder of horses, cattle, and fine sheep. An 1875 article in the *Sonoma Democrat* from Santa Rosa reported the ranch had about 500 head of cattle and 5,000 head of sheep not including the current year's crop of some 4,000 lambs. About 250 acres of grain had been planted, and a large amount of hay was to be cut also. The article reported "this fine farm is perhaps the largest body of the best class of agricultural land in one tract in the state."

Wilfred Page entertained guests and fellow thoroughbred horse-racing enthusiasts at his large home on Derby Lane and what is now Gravenstein Highway. The porch on the second floor went the whole length of the house, and spectators sat there to watch the races. The second story was removed in the 1930s by then owner, Giulio Castelli. (Courtesy of Frank Castelli.)

In 1892 the Page Brothers incorporated as the Cotati Company, listing as directors Charles, Wilfred, Arthur, and George Page, and John W. Mailliard, who was married to Lizzie Page. They had the ranch surveyed and had a town designed, and began offering lots for homes and small farms.

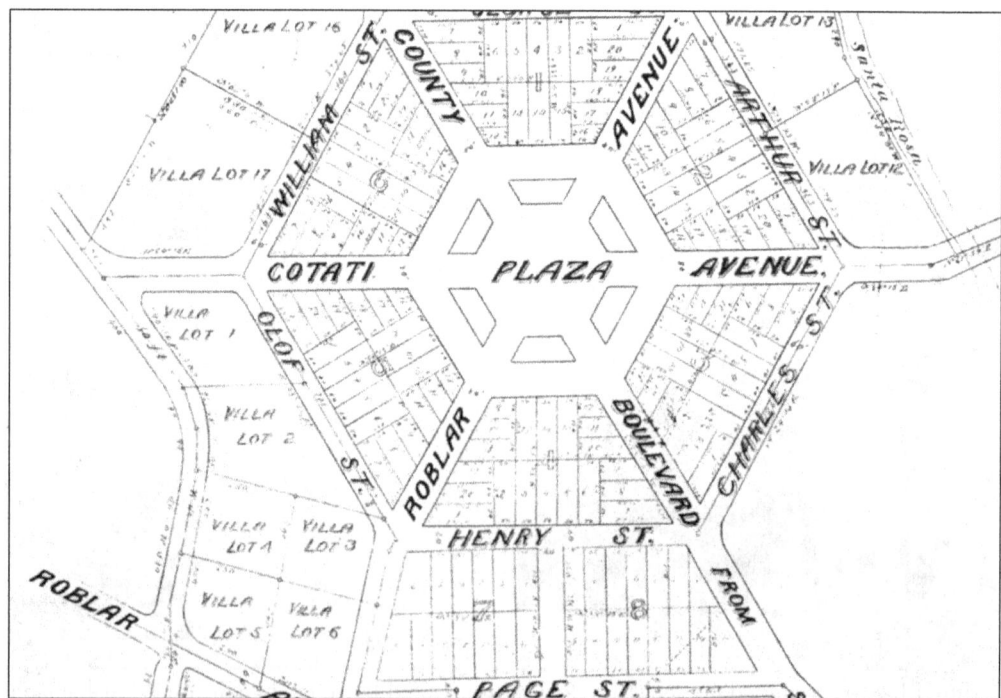

The center of the future town was the six-sided plaza, with the defining streets named for Wilfred Page's six brothers: Arthur, Charles, George, Henry, Olof, and William. Wilfred gave his own name to the avenue at the north end of the ranch.

The Cotati Plaza was dedicated by the Page family to public use. Before Cotati incorporated, the park was administered by the County of Sonoma. After incorporation, the board of supervisors granted it to the new city. On March 6, 1975, the California Landmarks Advisory Committee named the Cotati Plaza as a State Historical Landmark. Detroit, Michigan is the only other United States city with a hexagonal design.

A town needs a school, so the Page brothers donated land and built this one-room 20-by-40-foot school at the corner of what is now East School Street and West Sierra Avenue. The Cotati School District was established by the Sonoma County Board of Supervisors in 1893. Anna Elizabeth Dows taught all ages in one classroom. The Cotati Post Office was also established in 1893.

By the 1870s the San Francisco and Northwestern Railway had been built from Petaluma to Santa Rosa, and had two stops in the Cotate Ranch, Page's Station, and the Cotate Station. This depot, on the current East Cotati Avenue, was built in 1907, after the Cotati Progressive League, a committee of residents and businessmen, exerted pressure. (Courtesy of John R. Page.)

Travelers who came by rail to Cotati (the Pages had changed the spelling to make it easier to pronounce correctly) found an inviting vista and tempting "Land For Sale" signs as they left the train at East Cotati Avenue.

No. 21.   TIME SCHEDULE   No. 21.

TO TAKE EFFECT

On MONDAY, MAY 29, 1876, at 4 o'clock, A.M.,

For the government and information of employees only; the Company reserve the right to vary therefrom as circumstances may require.

TRAINS From San Francisco.				DISTANCE BETWEEN STATIONS.	DISTANCE FROM SAN FRANCISCO.	NAMES OF STATIONS.	DIST. FROM CLOVERDALE.	DISTANCE BETWEEN STATIONS.	TRAINS Towards San Francisco.			
No. 7. SUNDAY EXCURSION	No. 5. FREIGHT	No. 3. EXPRESS PASSENG'R	No. 1. MAIL AND PASSENG'R						No. 2. EXPRESS PASSENG'R	No. 4. MAIL AND PASSENG'R	No. 6. FREIGHT	No. 8. SUNDAY EXCURSION
8.00 A.M	....	3.00 P.M	7.00 A.M	....	....	SAN FRANCISCO (Green Street Wharf.)	90	34	12.25 P.M	8.00 P.M	....	7.20 P.M
10.00 "	2.00 P.M	5.00 "	9.00 "	34	34	DONAHUE	56	1	10.25 A.M	6.00 "	9.00 A.M	5 20 "
10.05 "	2.05* "	5.05 "	9.05 "	1	35	LAKEVILLE	55	7	10.18 "	5.55 "	8.40* "	5.15 "
10.20 "	2.45 "	5.25 "	9.20 "	7	42	PETALUMA	48	3	10.03 "	5.40 "	8.20 "	5.00 "
10.27* "	3.00* "	5.33* "	9.28* "	3	45	ELY'S	45	1	9.56* "	5.33 "	7.51* "	4.53* "
10.29* "	3.05* "	5 35* "	9.30* "	1	46	PENN'S GROVE	44	½	9.54* "	5 27* "	7.47* "	4.51* "
10.31* "	3.08* "	5.37* "	9.31* "	½	46½	GOODWIN'S	43½	2½	9.53* "	2.25* "	7.45* "	4.50* "
10 38* "	3.20* "	5.43* "	9.37* "	2½	49	PAGE'S	41	2½	9.48* "	5.19* "	7.35* "	4.44* "
10.44* "	3.32* "	5.49* "	9.43 "	2½	51½	COTATE RANCH	38½	2½	9.43 "	5.13* "	7.25* "	4.38* "
10.49* "	3 42* "	5.54* "	9.49* "	2½	54	OAK GROVE	36	3	9 34* "	5 07* "	7.17* "	4.32* "
11.00 "	4.05 "	6.04 "	10.00 "	3	57	SANTA ROSA	33	4	9.27 "	5.00 "	7.05 "	4.25 "
11.12 "	4.25* "	6.14 "	10.10 "	4	61	FULTON	29	2	9.17 "	4.48 "	6.35 "	4.12 "
11.17* "	4.43 "	6.19 "	10.15 "	2	63	MARK WEST	27	3	9.12 "	4.43 "	6.15* "	4.07* "
11.24 "	5.00 "	6.26 "	10.23 "	3	66	WINDSOR	24	4	9.05 "	4.35 "	6 00 "	4.00* "
11.36* "	5.20* "	6.36* "	10.33* "	4	70	GRANT'S	20	2	8.55* "	4.22* "	5.40* "	3.50* "
11.42 "	5.40 "	6.42 "	10.58 "	2	72	HEALDSBURG	18	4	8.50 "	4.15 "	5.30 "	3.45 "
11.52 "	6.00 "	6.52 "	10 48 "	4	76	LITTON'S SPRINGS	14	4	8.35 "	4.04 "	4.57 "	3.35 "
12.02 P.M	6.29* "	7.02 "	10.58 "	4	82	GEYSERVILLE	8	6	8.25 "	3.54 "	4.40 "	3.25 "
12.15* "	6.45 "	7 17* "	11.13* "	6	86	TRUETT'S	4	4	8.10* "	3.39* "	4.16* "	3.10* "
12.25 "	7.10 A.M	7.30 P.M	11.25 A.M	4	90	CLOVERDALE	....	....	8.00 A.M	3.30 P.M	4.00 A.M	3.00 P.M

FULTON AND GUERNEVILLE R. R.

SUNDAY EXCURSION		FREIGHT & PASSENG'R	FREIGHT & PASSENG'R	DIST'N STATS	FROM S.F.	NAMES OF STATIONS.	FROM GVLLE	DIST'N STATS	FREIGHT & PASSENG'R	FREIGHT & PASSENG'R		SUNDAY EXCURSION
11.15 A.M	....	6.20 P.M	10.20 A.M	2	61	FULTON	16	2	8.50 A.M	4.15 P.M	....	4.00 P.M
11.23 "	....	6.28 "	10.32 "	2	63	MEACHAM'S	14	4	8.36 "	4.02 "	....	3.51 "
11.39 "	....	6.50 "	10.56 "	4	67	LAGUNA	10	2	8.12 "	3.42 "	....	3.35 "
11.47 "	....	6.58 "	11.08 "	2	69	FORESTVILLE	8	2	8.00 "	3.30 "	....	3.27 "
11.55 "	....	7.08 "	11 20 "	2	71	GREEN VALLEY	6	3	7.48 "	3.18 "	....	3.15 "
12.07 M	....	7.30 P.M	11.40 A.M	3	74	KORBEL'S	3	3	7.30 A.M	3.00 P.M	....	3.00 P.M
....	....	....	....	3	77	GUERNEVILLE	....	....	....	....	....	....

NOTE.—Meeting and passing points are indicated by full-faced type; Flag stations by a *. Donahue, Santa Rosa, Windsor, Healdsburg, Cloverdale and Korbel's are regular wood and water stations. At Terminal Stations all Trains and Train Men will be under the immediate

In 1876 when this San Francisco and North Pacific Railroad schedule came out, the railroad stop on East Cotati Avenue was called Page's Station; the Cotate Ranch stop was at Wilfred Crossing.

The Page mansion is seen on the hilltop at the bottom of this aerial photo taken in the 1920s. The 75-acre orchard was planted to prunes and pears. Fred Keppel, who managed the ranch for the Pages at that time, predicted that the whole area would someday be planted with prunes.

The early ranchers worked hard, but they found time for music too. This band, called the Cotati Men of Melody, played at celebrations of all kinds, and members were described as looking very elegant in their white duck uniforms. Here the Men of Melody help dedicate the Odd Fellows Hall in 1911.

Two

ONE HUGE RANCH
BECOMES MANY
SMALL ONES

This giant chicken float fashioned from 15,000 white carnations won first prize for the Cotati Women's Improvement Club in Santa Rosa's Rose Parade in 1911. Edwin Keyt, standing, was one of the designers. The wings flapped, and with each flap children in chick outfits crowed. White Leghorns were the chickens of choice for most ranchers in the Cotati area, who raised them for eggs.

Emmanuel and Mary Trebino, pictured at left on their wedding day, came to Cotati in 1906 and settled on Helman Lane. They had three daughters, Josephine, Elizabeth, and Larraine. Removed to make way for the 101 freeway in 1955, the Trebino home was rebuilt, and still stands on land that is now part of South Sonoma Business Park. Elizabeth Trebino lived on the property until 2000. (Courtesy of Anita and Donald Ray.)

Emmanuel Trebino feeds his chickens. He also had about 15 milking cows, and sold eggs and milk. (Courtesy of Anita and Donald Ray.)

John and Mary Ann Amaral came to Cotati in 1906, and according to family lore, bought four parcels of land on what is now West Sierra Avenue for a $10 gold piece. They are pictured here with their son Anthony in 1904. Their granddaughter Dorothy Amaral Offutt still lives on the property. (Courtesy of Dorothy Offutt.)

Among the many immigrants who bought farms in Cotati were Henry Eickmeyer and his bride, Marie, from Germany. As was common for such couples, Henry came to America, worked for a few years, then went home to marry in 1914. He returned with his bride to start a new life. Their ranch was on Madrone Avenue. They are pictured here in 1920, with their son Henry, daughters Martha (on Marie's lap), and Lena (standing at right). (Courtesy of Lena Braden.)

Bernardo and Giustina Santero were born, reared, and married in Northern Italy. They came to Cotati in 1913, settling on a 15-acre farm on East Cotati Avenue. (Courtesy of Barney and Evelin Santero.)

John Santero, pictured with the family vegetable truck, was one of the eight children of Bernardo and Giustina Santero. The family raised a large variety of vegetables, which they sold door-to-door with a push cart in the early years, and later by truck. Carrots, beets, turnips, corn, and tomatoes were among the Santeros' crops. Several members of the family still live in Cotati, and all are ardent gardeners. They have been active in the Cotati Fire Department and Auxiliary, American Legion Post and Auxiliary, St. Joseph's Church, and other community organizations.

Fred Frengle developed a gas brooder stove, used to keep newly hatched chicks warm, that became very popular with chicken ranchers in the Petaluma-Cotati area and beyond. He established a factory and metal-working shop, and was later joined in the prosperous business by his son George.

This commercial structure on West Cotati Avenue (seen above when it was the Hub Cyclery) was built about 1930 by the Frengle family to house their metal shop. The front is tin-plated iron, molded to imitate stone. This building has had several uses over the years, is still standing, and in use now as the Whatever Hair and Nail Salon.

The Delevois Hatchery on the corner of what is now West Sierra Avenue and West School Street, was one of three hatcheries in Cotati serving the local ranchers and others outside the area. LaLomita Hatchery, operated by the Legarreta family, was on Madrone Avenue, and Cunningham Hatchery, owned by Andy Cunningham, was on Poplar Avenue. (Courtesy of Dee Sklavos.)

Chicken ranching was a family affair in Cotati in the early days. The Moon family had a ranch on the west side of town from 1914 to 1936, and their four daughters, from left to right, Celia, Martha, Georgia, and Florence, helped with the chores. (Courtesy of Flo Casarotti.)

(*Above*) Edwin N. Keyt, (standing at right) came to Cotati in 1906 and started a chicken ranch. In 1912 he launched a well drilling business, and in 1918 took his son Norton Keyt, seated on top of the drill rig, as his partner. George Mattson (left) was their assistant. (Courtesy of Bob and Mabel Nelson.)

Joe Rapoport and his wife, Sheba, came to Cotati in 1949, bought a run-down ranch on Cypress Avenue, and with the help of the Jewish community, improved it and learned to raise chickens. They had been active in Communist and Union politics in Europe and New York. (Courtesy of Lew Levinson.)

One of the largest agricultural operations in Cotati was the 127-acre Larsen dairy farm at the corner of Gravestein Highway and Stony Point Road. Henry and Marie Larsen operated it from 1947 to 1967, after which it was owned by their son Bob and his wife, Alice, who greatly expanded the dairy herd. Since 1973 they and their family have operated Larsen's Feed and Pet Supply Center on the same property.

Before the Cotati Public Utility District was formed in 1949 every home had a well, and well drillers were kept busy. Les Petersen, center, and Henry Wilfert, at left, were partners in this firm in 1946 that later became one of Cotati's largest businesses. Ken Hansen, their first employee, is at right. (Courtesy of Les Petersen.)

Frank Lund, son of pioneer residents Frands and Ann Lund, was able to make the heavy Cotati adobe soil produce, and he became a gladiolus hybridizer. He won many awards for his blossoms. His farm was on the old family ranch, along what is now Commerce Boulevard where Cotati Oaks Hardware now stands. (Courtesy of Janice Nelson.)

Sheep raised by Severa Wilford and his family brought home prizes to Cotati from local and state fairs for years. Pictured here with their Sonoma County Fair champion lambs are, from left to right, Severa Wilford Jr., S. Bud Wilford, and Art Nelson. (Courtesy of Janice Nelson.)

Many Japanese families settled in the Cotati area and operated successful chicken ranches. Pictured here in 1951 are the children of brothers Paul and James Otani, who ranched on Old Redwood Highway from 1938 to 1972. Their ranching was interrupted for five years during World War II, when they were sent to a relocation camp in Granada, Colorado. Pictured, from left to right, are Ruby, Kenny, Robert, Danny, and Pauline Otani. (Courtesy of Paul Otani.)

Chicken ranches could once be seen in all directions around Cotati. This one, operated by John and Ann McGorty, was in what is now the downtown area near the Plaza. (Courtesy of John McGorty.)

John and Else Christensen established this chicken ranch in the 1920s on East School Street where the Oak Knoll subdivision is now. The Christensens and their five children operated the ranch until the late 1990s. (Courtesy of Christine Sims Myers.)

Members of the Christensen family are pictured here, from left to right, in 1960: (front row) Anna Marie Christensen, Else Christensen, Christine Sims, and Nancy Sims; (back row) John Christensen Sr., Louis Christensen, and wife Helene, John Christensen Jr., Karen Christensen, Agnete Christensen Sims, Raymond Sims, and Raylene Christensen. (Courtesy of Christine Sims Myers.)

Three

A COMMUNITY
DEVELOPS

This view of the Cotati countryside along what is now West Sierra Avenue shows typical small farms that developed after 1893. The Page brothers, operating as the Cotati Company, had commissioned George Tyler Trowbridge, and later David W. Batchelor, to sell hundreds of 5- to 20-acre farms to new settlers. The Cotati Company offered low-interest loans, and Petaluma feed merchants welcomed new farmers with credit. The community became a melting pot of different nationalities as energetic immigrants sought their fortune on family farms.

William and Jennie Wilford came to Cotati in 1904 and bought property. Their home, shown here, was on Cypress Avenue near West Railroad Avenue. Their son Severa married Anne Lund, the daughter of Frands and Rose Lund, who had come to Cotati in 1894 from Oakland, and were among the first wave of new settlers. Lund had jumped off a train and walked across fields and a stream to the Page ranch house to find out how to buy land. They were typical of the new settlers, whom Wilfred Page described as "people of a good class, which will make very desirable citizens." (Courtesy of Janice Nelson.)

Anne Lund and Severa Wilford are pictured here on their wedding day in 1918. Two days later he left for the Army in World War I. Anne Lund Wilford, born in 1897, was proud in 1978 to be the oldest living Cotati-born citizen. The couple lived in town all their lives, raised their family, and conducted their ranching business here. (Courtesy of Janice Nelson.)

The Congregational Church of Cotati began with a congregation of 13 residents in 1901, meeting in the rear of a local store. They raised $100 in gold coin to purchase a lot from the Cotati Company on the corner of what is now West Sierra Avenue and Page Street, and built this redwood church in 1907. It is still a busy and well-loved church and a Cotati landmark.

A blacksmith shop had been one of the earliest businesses in Cotati and it found customers among the new farmers. Fred Keppel, who later became manager of the Page ranch, came to town as a blacksmith in 1906 and operated this shop on LaPlaza Street in 1906.

St. Joseph's Catholic Church began as a mission in 1908 when members set about raising funds to build a church. By November of the same year they had raised $1,650 to build this 150-seat church on the corner of William Street and what is now West Cotati Avenue. It still stands and now serves a large congregation as the Korean Baptist Church.

The Cotati Women's Improvement Club was established in 1909, when members began raising money to build a community clubhouse. The first section of the hall was finished a year later, and in ensuing years, more wings were added. The building is still a gathering place in the Plaza, now as Ner Shalom Synagogue.

The Loyal Cotati Lodge, Manchester Unity #8177, International Order of Odd Fellows (IOOF), was established in 1910. In 1911 they constructed this meeting hall at the corner of William Street and the former County Boulevard, now Old Redwood Highway. The lodge sold the hall in 1957, and it was extensively restored in 1969 by real estate broker and auctioneer Joe Dorfman, who had his offices there. It is still in use as business offices. (Courtesy of Lillian Jasperson.)

Among the IOOF members sharing a chicken pot pie dinner about 1920 are, on far left, from front to back, John DeBorba, John Klinkenberg, George Anderson, Jack Scriver, Bill Blodgett, John Santero, and Cecil Ross. Frank Cullen sits at right front. (Courtesy of Barney and Evelin Santero.)

Robert C. Ross came to Cotati after his book store in San Francisco was lost in the earthquake and fire of 1906. In 1909 he bought the general store, and began expanding the business. He also became the postmaster and had the post office in his store. He carried food and hardware, poultry supplies, and had an egg receiving and candling department. He was active in Cotati organizations, such as the Lions Club and IOOF Lodge. He and his first wife had three children, and after his wife died, Ross married Helen Jamieson, with whom he had a daughter, Lillian. (Courtesy of Lillian Jasperson.)

The Ross Store, once on the corner of LaPlaza and what is now West Sierra Avenue, offered just about everything needed by man, beast, or chicken. An early Cotati historian credited Ross for lifting the local business scene out of stagnation. Postcards that Robert Ross once offered for sale are a major source of photographic history today.

The Ross egg and poultry business operated out of a group of small buildings behind Robert Ross' store. Later this phase of the business was handled by the Poultry Producers of Central California, which occupied a store adjacent to the Ross Store. (Courtesy of Lillian Jasperson.)

An unidentified customer (left) with a thirst is served by Mrs. Brooks and Mr. Churchill at the Ross Store soda fountain.

Robert Ross also entertained Cotatians with this movie theater, where his son Cecil showed silent films accompanied by Mrs. Ross on the piano. It was located on what is now West Sierra Avenue and is still in use as Finer Perceptions used book store.

The Ross family lived in this handsome home on West Sierra Avenue adjacent to the Ross businesses. It is still a residence today. Note the windmill at left, a common sight in Cotati before the days of public utilities.

Several small stores occupied the streets around the Plaza. This view, *c.* 1915, looking north shows the Park Store and Halley's General Store. LaPlaza was not paved, stores had wooden sidewalks, and the Plaza had several large oak trees. None of these buildings are still standing. (Courtesy of Syd Lundgren.)

This *c.* 1920 view, looking south on LaPlaza, shows the Ross businesses, Moore's Garage, and the Cotati Hotel on the corner of La Plaza and what is now Old Redwood Highway. These buildings have all been replaced with more modern structures.

G.A. Lau operated this general store along the railroad tracks on the north side of East Cotati Avenue. Lau also was the station manager when the railroad depot was built in 1907.

G.A. Lau built this general merchandise store on LaPlaza about 1918. It continued as a grocery and general merchandise store under various owners until the 1960s.

John Lopus built the Cotati Hotel in 1911. It was described in newspapers as "one of the best hostelries in the county, with large rooms, newly furnished, a first class barber shop and public baths." Mrs. Lopus supervised the dining room. The hotel changed hands several times over the years, but always was a favorite stopping place for visitors and traveling businesspeople. It was said to be especially popular as a speakeasy during Prohibition.

The Cotati French Laundry was located on West Cotati Avenue west of the Plaza near the corner of El Rancho Drive in the 1920s. It might be assumed that Dr. Thomas Page's family, who lived in the mansion on the hill nearby, were among its clients. This building later housed a newspaper, but no longer exists.

Olson's Meat Market and Curtis Egg Dealer were located on the east side of the Plaza in 1918. Neither of these buildings is still standing.

Mrs. Olson worked with her husband, Hans "Ole" Olson, in the meat market and was said to be a very strong woman. Mr. Olson was active in the Cotati Lions Club, Cotati Chamber of Commerce, and Odd Fellows Lodge.

Southwest of the Plaza along El Rancho Drive, there was once a handsome grove of trees known as Cotati Oaks. It was a favored spot for picnics, like the one pictured here on July 4, 1911. In the middle background Congressman Clarence Lea is seen orating, and to his right is a glimpse of the Page mansion on the hill.

Children celebrated the glorious Fourth of July with tug-of-war contests and sack races. They especially enjoyed sliding down the hill over the smooth dry grass on sleds that were pulled to the top by mules.

With the town growing rapidly, the old one-room school was soon outgrown. In 1905 a matching section with belltower was added to house two teachers and their classes. A rolling door connected the two classrooms. Cotati School included junior high school classes until 1948, when the school voted to send older students to Petaluma Junior High.

By 1913 the school was again outgrown, and this school, designed by Petaluma architect Brainerd Jones, was built by Penngrove contractor Al Hermann. It was described as one of the most modern and beautiful schools in Sonoma County. The old school was moved to the Page Ranch property on West Cotati Avenue and used as a hay barn.

On Valentine's Day, 1921, the eight-year-old Cotati School was destroyed by a fire that was apparently started by an exploding boiler. Students arrived the next morning to find their school a smoking ruin. Classes met in the Women's Clubhouse, IOOF Hall, Congregational Church hall, and other spaces while a new school was built.

The new school was built on the same site, at the corner of West School Street and West Sierra, and opened in 1922. Students are pictured here doing morning exercises. This building, abandoned by the school district in 1971, became Cotati City Hall.

American Legion Cotati Post 10, founded soon after World War I, is still active today. For years the organization sponsored dances at the Women's Clubhouse that were major social events in central Sonoma County. Among other activities, the Post provided the 60-foot flagpole in the Cotati Plaza. Pictured here are members who were honored in 1971 for 45- and 50-year memberships; they are, from left to right, (front row) Severa L. Wilford Sr. and Robert P. Wolbert, both 50-year members; (back row) Jack Flottman, Herman Levy, Anton Jorgensen, Milt Palmgren, Anthony Hahn, Al Hillendahl, Lorenzo Saccato, and Claudio Falletti, all 45-year members. (Courtesy of American Legion Post 103.)

Officers of Cotati American Legion Post 103 and its Ladies Auxiliary posed at a ceremony in the 1950s. Pictured are, from left to right, (front row) Anne Wilford, Evelyn Johnstone, Dorothy Offutt, Peggy Boysen, Evelin Santero, Doris Vesgaard, Mary Peterson, Agnes Olsen, Marguerite Pavlou, and Florence Jensen; (back row) Leona Wilford, Georgina Petersen, Tony Miranda, unidentified, Mickey McKay, Jerry Jensen, Nick Wodrich, Lloyd Winter, and Barney Santero. (Courtesy of Barney and Evelin Santero.)

Four

THE AUTO
YEARS

In the early days, the main road through Cotati, mostly unpaved, was called Cotati Boulevard by local residents. In 1915 residents donated rights-of-way and money to persuade the State of California to choose Cotati as the main route between Petaluma and Santa Rosa. In the past Petaluma Hill Road and Stony Point Road had been the routes of choice. With a state highway through the middle of town, Cotati became a popular stop for the motoring public. Service stations, garages, and restaurants began to appear among the feed stores and general merchandise emporiums.

Cotati Garage was one of the first businesses to offer help for auto drivers. Owned by brothers Sophus and Joe Jensen, it was located near the Plaza and no longer exists.

George E. Moore built this large garage at the southeast corner of LaPlaza and Redwood Highway after his previous blacksmith shop and garage near the Ross Store on LaPlaza was destroyed in 1926 in a spectacular fire that threatened the entire downtown area. The extent of the damage, and a serious wreck of a Santa Rosa fire truck that had raced to the rescue, led to the development of the Cotati Volunteer Fire Department. Robert Ross bought the old property to expand his business—and protect himself from garage fires. George Moore and his family lived upstairs in the new garage and were prominent citizens. In addition to selling and servicing cars, in 1932 he handled airplanes and could arrange flying lessons. This building has had many uses over the years and is still standing, now housing Tradewinds Tavern, Nicolino's Restaurant, and Las Manos clothing store.

Jack Hahn is pictured driving a 1918 Cadillac converted into a fire truck with an old chemical tank. It was one of the first vehicles owned by the Cotati Fire Department after it was organized in 1927. There were ten volunteer members, and fire protection was financed by a donation of $2.30 by every property owner, plus money raised at dances.

By 1941 The Cotati Fire Department boasted an assortment of fire-fighting equipment, some purchased with funds raised by its Women's Auxiliary through card parties and dances. A new modern fire station was built on the same site on LaPlaza in 1991. In 1993 the Cotati department merged with the Penngrove Fire Department to form Rancho Adobe Fire Department.

Pictured in front of the firehouse in the Plaza in 1955 are most of the volunteer firemen, by then many more than the ten in the original department. Pictured, from left to right, are Chief Burt Chadwick, Nick Wodrich, Ralph McGinnis (assistant chief), Walt Jagla, Joe Biscarret, Tubby Braden, Barney Santero, Alvin Olsen, Steve Castelli, George Frengle, Clarence Christiansen, Henry Eickmeyer, Clyde Skilling, Les Offutt, Hank Aguirre, and Adolph (Curley) Carli. Most of the volunteers worked at nearby businesses or farms, and when the fire siren blew, they left whatever they were doing to race to the firehouse.

Burt Chadwick (left) was one of early Cotati's best-known citizens. He was one of the founders of the Cotati Volunteer Fire Department and was its chief from 1919 to 1967. His bar and barber shop were across the street from the fire station, and if the siren blew Burt would leave a client half-shaved or drinks half-poured when he dashed to answer the fire call. He is pictured here on the department's 40th anniversary, with Assistant Chief Ralph McGinnis, who succeeded him as chief. (Courtesy of Bud Chadwick.)

This combination pool hall/barber shop owned by Walt Woolery was on LaPlaza Street, between the Cotati Hotel and the blacksmith shop. Woolery also managed the Cotati baseball team, which competed against teams from other towns.

In 1932, Charles and Yetta Wedel, who had bought the old Cotati Hotel ten years earlier, moved it back and built this modern restaurant. Right alongside the new state highway, it was famous for its duck dinners, and had a large duck pond next to it. When the state chose the route as the Redwood Highway in 1915, property owners were encouraged to use Spanish-style architecture in all new semi-public buildings. The Cotati Inn was considered the ultimate in elegance in its day. It later became Sophie's, Michel's, and in 1968 became the famed Inn of the Beginning. The building is now occupied by Sweet Lou's Restaurant, Fran the Sandalady, and Spancky's Tavern.

In 1920 a builder and promoter named Jack S. Prince created more excitement than Cotati had ever known when he convinced racing enthusiasts and investors all over the North Bay area that he could build a world-class auto speedway. He succeeded on 135 acres on East Cotati Avenue alongside the railroad tracks building a huge oval track that became known as the Cotati Speedway.

The all-wood, bowl-shaped track, 1.25 miles around, required over 3 million feet of lumber. It also contained over 70 tons of 20-penny spikes and over 100 kegs of 10- and 12-penny nails.

The Cotati Speedway's surface was constructed of two-by-three-inch planks, laid on edge, as smoothly finished as a bowling alley. As the track began to take shape, local car buffs posed for publicity photos to help promote sale of life memberships in the endeavor, and 150 carpenters poured in from all directions to keep construction moving at a rapid pace. Groundbreaking was held on April 24, 1921 and the grand opening only four months later, on August 14. The Cotati Speedway was on the same circuit as Indianapolis, and world record–breaking races were expected. Tommy Milton, who had won the last classic at Indianapolis, was scheduled to race driving a Durant Special.

This poster for the Cotati Speedway's second season was typical of the publicity that drew fans from a wide area.

Eddie Hearne, driving his Disteel Duesenberg, won the first race at the Cotati Speedway and set a new world record, driving 150 miles in 1 hour, 21 minutes, and $16^{1}/_{5}$ seconds, averaging 110.84 miles per hour. He won $5,000.

Eddie Miller, driving a Duesenberg, was one of the stars of the first race. Even with a flat tire he still came in fourth with a time of 1 hour, 29 minutes, $58^{1}/_{5}$ seconds. Roscoe Sarles was second; Tommy Milton, third; Alton Soules, fifth; and Joe Thomas, sixth. Newspapers in the vicinity ran contests offering fans prizes for picking which drivers would be ahead as they finished each lap.

At the first race on August 14, 1921, all seats were filled and some 10,000 people jammed the inner field. It was a clear, balmy day and no problems were reported. It seemed that Jack Prince's predictions had come true. People who had bought life memberships were delighted, but the first profits went to pay off Prince's building expenses. Two weeks later professional motorcycle races were held on the track, and Otto Walker drove his Harley-Davidson to set a national record for a 25-mile race, finishing in 16.29 minutes, an average of 106 miles per hour in spite of a blown-out tire.

Racers and their crews posed at the Cotati Speedway. An estimated 20,000 people witnessed the first race. The Northwestern Pacific Railroad ran special trains for fans, and San Francisco Bay ferries were taxed beyond capacity. Spectators arrived in some 8,000 cars and main roads as well as dirt side roads were clogged with traffic for hours after the race.

Wonders of the Cotati Speedway and the need for more highways vied for top billing in major newspapers in the San Francisco Bay Area.

On a sunny day, the speedway was a wonderful place. After the first race, however, cold, rainy weather, and traffic congestion resulted in dwindling crowds. After only its second season the track was abandoned as a financial failure, and life membership investors were furious. The record-breaking "fastest track in the world" had lasted only two years. The Speedway was dismantled and the lumber sold to pay outstanding bills. Much of it went to build homes and businesses in the Cotati area.

The Fox Garage, on what is now Old Redwood Highway, catered to racers, and even changed its name to lure them. This building, still standing, has been a feed store and now houses Arch's Glass Co, Kay's Photo, and Miller Driving School.

Fred Keppel, manager of the Cotati Land Company for the Page family, fed deer in a park in part of the Plaza. The plaza deer became a tourist attraction. One night during World War II, with meat rationing enforced, a rustler broke down the fence and stole the deer. In the 1950s citizen volunteers formed the Keep the Plaza Green Club to improve and maintain the park.

Airplanes became a familiar sight in the 1920s, landing in the broad, open fields of the Cotati Ranch. Landing areas were rotated according to where crops were being grown. Aviators said the atmosphere in the area was unusually free of air pockets, and Cotati Company pilots would take youths for $2 sightseeing rides. In 1932 Ted Peoples offered flying lessons in a new Curtiss-Wright Mona Coupe, and had several eager students.

Seeding and dusting were frequently done by plane in the hay fields and later seed farm fields north of town. Tom Insall, a well-known master at this craft, frequently buzzed the community. Bob Chadwick, pictured here about 1948, worked for Insall.

Cotati Fire Department had a hot baseball team in the 1940s. Pictured here are, from left to right, (front row) Ralph McGinnis, Steve Castelli, Clyde Skilling, Carl Eickmeyer, and Henry Eickmeyer; (back row) Burt Chadwick, Nick Wodrich, Tubby Braden, Jack Hahn, Les Offutt, and Frank Ferrero.

Nort Keyt enjoyed boxing, and had a gym in his well-drilling shop where he gave lessons to other young men. Pictured, from left to right, are (seated) Art Nusselbaum, unidentified, Dick Greenhouse, Harry Mortimer, and Sugar; (standing) Bud Wilford, Nort Keyt, Shorty VanSlanelts, Jim Veronda, Isabel Olsen, and unidentified. (Courtesy of Bob and Mabel Nelson.)

Isabel Amaral and her husband, Tony, had a ranch across the street from the Cotati School. She was much loved by students because she operated a small snack bar where she served hamburgers, hot dogs, and assorted goodies to children during their lunch break. (Courtesy of Dorothy Offutt.)

Cotati School Blue Bell baseball team posed with their teacher in 1923. Pictured, from left to right, are (front row) Arnold Rimer, Peter Santero, James Veronda, Frank Yriberry; (middle row) Evin McClean, Cedric Bourboulis, George Mattson, and Miguel Yriberry; (back row) Ted Schindler, George Cross, Miss Ball, and Edward Duscharm.

The highway running through town made a perfect track for runners. This Cotati team in a 10-mile marathon about 1920 included, from left to right, Jim Veronda, Al Peters, four unidentified runners, and Ray Skilling.

Posing on the front steps of the Cotati School in 1921 are, from left to right, (front row) Emilie Alvoaza, Herbert Frengle, Elisa Loustalot, Flora Moon, Walter Christiansen, and Mildred Wright; (middle row) Willie Lahti, Rosa Aguirre, Maxie Aguirre, Jimmy Malley, ? Davidson, Ida Tompkins, George Stack, Jack Richardson, and Francis Jensen; (back row) Ingrie Sarlin, Hattie Widlund, Elmer Tillman, Lillian Besso, Regina Brennan, Dorothy Stack, Florence Sell, Lela Reidel, Antoinette B?, Robert Ross, John DeBorba, Walter Christensen, Charlie P?, and Peter Boysen. This photo was taken a short time before this school was destroyed by fire.

High on a hill above Poplar Avenue, Mr. and Mrs. K. Lahti opened a swimming pool and recreational facility in June 1922. The concrete pool, measuring 30 by 70 feet and 7 feet deep at one end, became immediately popular.

The Lahti pool boasted 40 private dressing rooms, two large steam baths, and a dance hall with an electric player piano. The owners sold sandwiches and soft drinks and rented bathing suits. People were lined up daily awaiting dressing rooms and many local children learned to swim here. The business collapsed after Mr. and Mrs. Lahti had serious differences that led to a well plugged with concrete and a home burned.

Pia and Giocondo (George) Benedetti, pictured on their wedding day in 1913 in Lucca, Tuscany, Italy, lived in Sonoma and Santa Rosa before coming to Cotati in 1927. The family, which grew to include a daughter, Millie, and two sons, Gene and Dan, bought the 14-acre ranch where the Lahti pool had been. The family had the well cleaned and used lumber from the old dressing rooms and dance hall to build their first home. Benedetti raised cattle and chickens. In the summer the Benedetti children would fill the old pool with water, and enjoy a swim. (Courtesy of Millie Libarle.)

A Christmas play for the American Legion Auxiliary in the 1950s featured Herb Winter, front, and in back, from left to right, Whitey Waldron, Joe Biscarret, Howard Sisk, Wanda Biscarret, Bobby Waldron, Nick Wodrich, Dorothy Offutt (in cat suit) Zanette Brown, Jerry Jensen, and Jean Winter. (Courtesy of Dorothy Offutt and Evelin Santero.)

When Al and Jennie Falletti came home from their honeymoon in 1948 they moved into this brand new house on the corner of West Sierra and Olof Street, part of the chicken ranch of Jennie's parents, Pete and Elizabeth Veronda. It was built by Bill Budinsky, a local contractor, with brickwork done by Jake Veronda, Jennie's cousin. The Fallettis immediately started landscaping, and the home is still known for its beautiful gardens. (Courtesy of Jennie Falletti.)

Five

PROUD TO BE THE "HUB OF SONOMA COUNTY"

Cotati businesses were expanding by the 1940s and the people were proud of their little town. Every parade for miles around had a float from Cotati, and many parades wound their way through Cotati streets too. This entry in a Petaluma parade featured local girls representing Cotati businesses.

Clyde Skilling opened the Cotati Pharmacy, shown here, on what is now Old Redwood Highway in 1932. Later he bought what had once been the Cotati Hardware Store (at far right) and moved his pharmacy there. In 1929 Robert C. and Ethel Clothier opened the Cotati Realty Company in a small office near the hotel; then moved to the building shown here, and later to one on the corner of Charles Street as their business expanded.

Robert and Ethel Clothier, pictured here in 1952, became Cotati's most enthusiastic supporters. She was not only a businesswoman but a mother of two, Camp Fire leader, club member, and newspaper reporter. He was postmaster for 15 years. Together they operated the Greyhound Bus Agency, Western Union, and State Fish and Game license bureau. Clothier was instrumental in forming the Cotati Public Utility District, which gave the town safe water and sewage disposal, and was one of the first advocates of incorporation. (Courtesy of Marguerite Revard.)

During a wartime blackout in April 1945, the Jensen Brothers' Garage on what is now Old Redwood Highway in the center of Cotati's main business block burned in a late night fire. Through the heroic efforts of Cotati firemen and mutual aid from volunteers and other fire departments, the fire was contained. Since the garage was next to the O'Brien Paint Factory (far left) this was a close call for downtown Cotati.

Pictured *c.* 1950, O'Brien Empire Paint, the only family owned paint manufacturing plant in Northern California, was first owned by Harry DeGregory, who sold it to Bill O'Brien in July 1944. O'Brien had been affiliated with Fuller Paint for 19 years. This building has seen many changes of use but is still standing. The landmark paint can was removed in the 1960s.

Irving Lipton bought the Skilling Pharmacy on what is now Old Redwood Highway in 1941, and offered a variety of groceries, medicines, and a lunch counter/soda fountain that became a popular town gathering place. This building, having seen many changes, is still in use as the Redwood Cafe.

Robert and Ethel Clothier bought this building at the corner of Charles Street and what is now Old Redwood Highway, which had been a garage and Rayburn's Grocery, about 1940. They converted it to house their Cotati Realty office, the post office, the Greyhound ticket station, and an Exchange Bank branch. It was later the Cotati Co-op Grocery and is now Tama-Rama's. (Courtesy of Marguerite Revard.)

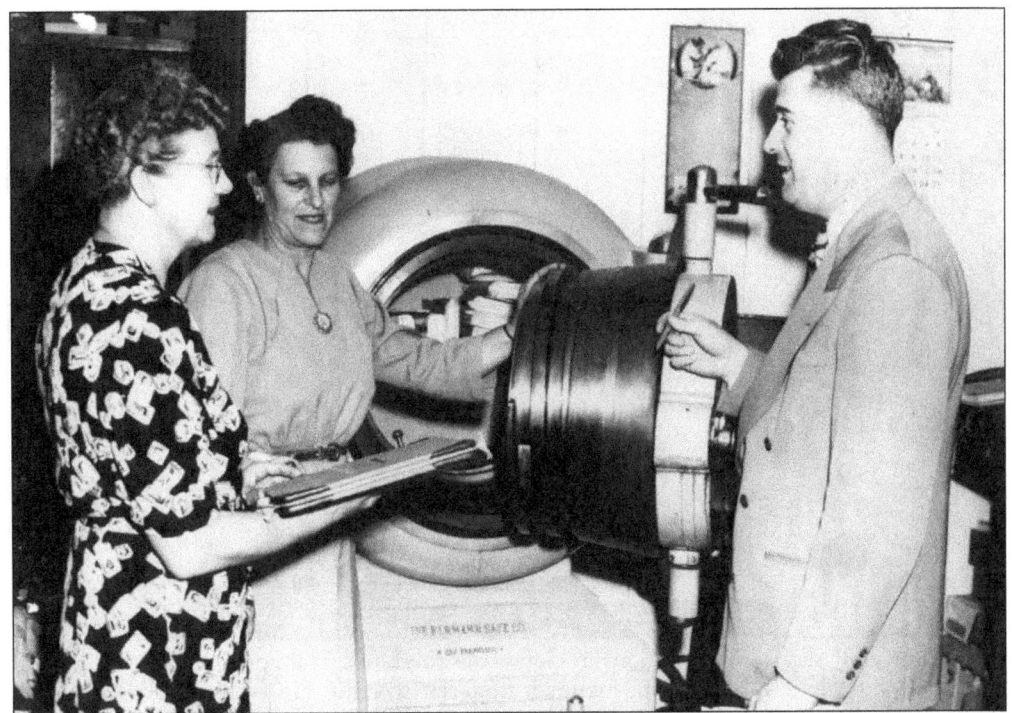

The Cotati branch of the Exchange Bank opened in Cotati on December 29, 1941, in a portion of the Clothier Building. Pictured about 1948 are staff members, from left to right, Gladys Giddings Starnes, Waunoma Tonelli, and John Guaspari. The bank moved to a new building on Old Redwood Highway in the 1950s and is still operating there.

Frizelle-Enos Feed Co. had a retail store on Old Redwood Highway and this mill on East Cotati Avenue near the railroad tracks. The mill burned in a spectacular fire in 1952, but was replaced with a building that is now a glass company.

One of the early service organizations in Cotati was the Lions Club, pictured here in 1930 in the old Cotati Hotel dining room. Pictured, from left to right, are (seated) Clarence Eales, three unidentified men, Bob Clothier, and standing, Arnold Wessels, Yetta and Charles Wedel (owners of the hotel), A.J. Petersen, several unidentified men, Burt Chadwick (third from right), Hans Olson, and unidentified. The Cotati Lions are still active. Pictured, from left to right, are (seated at left) Clarence Eales, three unidentified men, Bob Clothier, and unidentified; (standing) Arnold Wessels, Yetta and Charles Wedel (owners of the hotel), A.J. Petersen, and several unidentified people; (seated at right) several unidentified men, Burt Chadwick (third from right), and Hans Olson (second from right).

In 1947 it was not at all unusual to come downtown on horseback, as Phyllis Donahue, seen here, illustrates. The Cotati Club was on LaPlaza, across from the firehouse.

The Cotati Grange was an active community service organization during the 1940s, 1950s, and 1960s, and mock weddings were a favorite kind of entertainment. Taking part in this skit, from left to right, are (front row) Margaret Richardson, unidentified, Sylvia Moyle, Beatrice Atkinson, and unidentified; (back row) Creig George, Ralph Day, Tom Moyle, and Lawrence Atkinson.

The Cotati Chapter of Native Daughters of the Golden West was established December 2, 1948, and became one of the very active organizations in the mid-20th century. Celebrating the installation of Zanette Brown, from left to right, are (front row) Marge Rosselli, Marie Baranzini, visiting deputy, Zanette Brown, Cora Brown, Ursula Lucchesi, and Amelia Larsen; (back row) Florence Jensen, Violet McKean, Lois Boerstler, Evelyn Johnstone, visiting deputy, Pat Taddie, Edna Chandler, Christine Matteri, Lois Olsen, and Margaret Woodward.

E.A. Little, better known as "Colonel," pictured here with his dogs, established a weekly newspaper, *The Cotatian*, in 1944. Several weeklies had previously been started in Cotati, *The Lancer*, edited by Ted Schindler, was followed by *The Record*, also a weekly, in 1931. Its publisher, E.J. Halcrow, ceased publication in June of the same year. Colonel Little was one of the breed of traveling newspapermen who specialized in launching small town papers, then moved on to new adventures. He sold *The Cotatian* to Brent Payne, who later sold it to Ed and Helen Runyon.

This building on West Cotati Avenue, formerly the Cotati Laundry, was the office of *The Cotatian* from 1944 to 1954, when the newspaper moved to part of the former O'Brien Paint Company building on Old Redwood Highway. It is no longer standing.

Ed and Helen Runyon purchased *The Cotatian* in 1947. They also owned weekly newspapers in Penngrove, Forestville, and Middletown. Their nephew, Lloyd Draper, came to work for them in 1948, after Air Corps service during World War II.

The authors, Lloyd Draper and his wife, Prue, purchased *The Cotatian* from the Runyons in 1951, and published the paper until 1964, when they sold it to Sheldon Sackett. It merged with the *Rohnert Park Press*, and had several changes of name in the following years. Several other small weeklies were published in Cotati in the 1970s including the *Cotati Call* and the *Bugle*.

Dr. Herbert C. Honor and his wife, Dr. Vera Ocker Honor, also a physician, came to Cotati about 1932. Cotati's first doctor had been Dr. Loftus Harlan Francis, who had his office in a two-story house on what is now Old Redwood Highway. The Doctors Honor had their offices above the Ross Store, on the corner of LaPlaza and what is now West Sierra Avenue. They left in 1940 to serve as hospital doctors in the Philippines, and were later taken as prisoners of war by the Japanese there. They are pictured here in their Philippine finery, with their daughter Dorothy and son, whose name is unknown. They later returned to the United States, but not to Cotati. (Courtesy of Lillian Jasperson.)

Dr. John Roberts came to Cotati in 1948 and, except for a few years during the Korean War when he was drafted, he served the community for 40 years. His family grew up in town and most remain in the Cotati area. He was active in many community service organizations, and was instrumental in the incorporation of the City of Cotati. He was still in active practice in Cotati when he died in an auto accident in 1988. (Courtesy of Rick Roberts.)

Pictured here riding in a float entered by the Petaluma Co-operative Creamery (now Clover Milk Company) in a Cotati procession about 1952 are Diane and Joanne Johnson. The elaborate telephone pole in the background was provided by the Rural Telephone Co., owned by A.J. and W.J. Guglielmetti, which served Cotati from 1904 to 1949, when Pacific Telephone took over.

St. Joseph's Catholic Church began holding chicken and beef barbeques in 1940 as family events for parishoners. After World War II, the events were made public, and for over ten years they were the community's most popular festivals, drawing about 5,000 people. Here Beverly Hahn, left, and Doreen Ferrero publicize the event.

Parades have always been among Cotati's favorite events, and this one on LaPlaza at the St. Joseph's Barbecue drew a big crowd. Glenn Nylander clowns with the antique firetruck. Seen in the background, Ferrero's General Store was a well-known shopping and gathering place.

Although the annual barbecues in the Plaza were sponsored by St. Joseph's Church, everyone in town pitched in to help dig the pit, wrap the beef for the cooking, and prepare the chickens, salads, and desserts that were served. Planning for the events took months, and preparations lasted almost a week. Standing in the center of the front row in this photo is Sam Houser, who later became Cotati's first mayor.

Lois Olsen, at left, and Linnie Pushard, at right, were among the Cotatians who staffed an aircraft observation post during World War II and again in the 1950s. Volunteers worked shifts to provide lookout 24 hours a day, reporting all planes that flew over Cotati. Planes from the Naval Auxiliary Air Station north of town and crop-dusters for the seed farm complicated their task.

One of Cotati's most dedicated citizens was Marguerite Hahn, who moved to town after marrying Jack Hahn in 1933. She worked with the Fire Department Auxiliary, Red Cross, at the Civil Defense air observation post, chamber of commerce, St. Joseph's Church, and several youth organizations. She was also the town librarian, and for 33 years the town's newspaper correspondent. She seemed to be everywhere, taking photographs and writing for all the papers in the area. She died suddenly in 1972 at the age of 65, while talking on the telephone about a news story.

The U.S. Navy established the Cotati Auxiliary Air Station in 1943, to be used for aircraft carrier landing practice. It had barracks for eight men, a control tower, and a garage. Neighbors in the Helman Lane/Lowell Avenue area were fascinated by the "touch and go" maneuvers practiced by Navy pilots on the two runways. This land is now covered by the shopping areas and residences of Rohnert Park. (Courtesy of Syd Lundgren.)

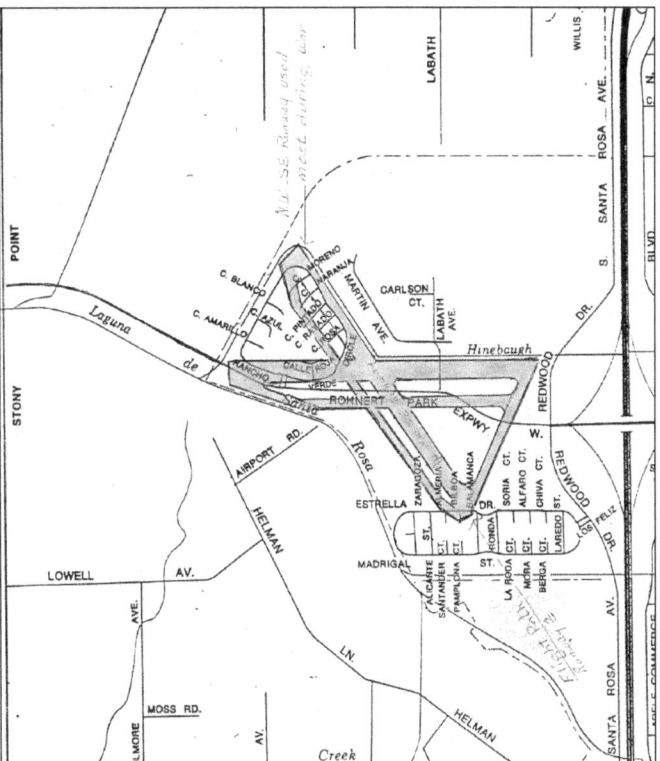

Beginning in 1954, the old Navy runways became the Cotati Raceways, and were used for auto racing, first by the Street Angels and later by Sports Car Club of America. Actress Jayne Mansfield reigned as queen of the races at this event on September 10 and 11, 1960, sponsored by the Northern California Corvette Association.

As in other American cities, drive-in restaurants were favorite gathering places in Cotati. Jensen's Country Inn, also called the Surrey Inn in the 1940s and 1950s when it had a surrey perched on its roof, was on Gravenstein Highway at Stony Point Road. The building is still standing.

This drive-in at Gravenstein intersection pictured in 1998, began as Morrow's in the 1940s. It was later owned by Whitey Waldron, and after 1954, by John Curtis. In recent years it was owned by Eugene Balter, but the building is no longer in existence. Tubby's is now on East Cotati Avenue.

Cotati Chamber of Commerce was the main voice of the town before incorporation as a city. Pictured here c. 1955 are, from left to right, (front row) Sophie Gwerder, William O'Brien (president), and Mary Sisk (treasurer); (back row) Elmer Chadwick, Marguerite Hahn, Sam Smith, Clifford Macklin, Dr. Robert Quimby, Harold Taylor, Howard Sisk, and Robert VanBreen.

Bill Kortum, DVN, launched his veterinary practice in Cotati in the 1950s, and was one of the town's most farsighted and hard-working citizens. As president of the chamber of commerce he led the drive to get Cotati's site chosen for a new state college, and was a leader in the effort to incorporate the City of Cotati. He was later elected Sonoma County supervisor, and has led statewide environmental conservation efforts from his home in Petaluma for over half a century.

Cotati had a library from 1910, when Charles Page donated his book collection to the town, until 1976, when the Sonoma County Public Library administration moved the branch to Rohnert Park. Pictured here *c.* 1960 are Adelaide McClure, left, assistant librarian, and Marguerite Hahn, librarian. The last Cotati Library branch was in a small building on Old Redwood Highway now occupied by Gravenstein Travel.

Frank Dolinsek found the Cotati soil and climate perfect for propagating prize-winning tuberous begonias in the 1960s and 1970s. His large greenhouses, located on Gravenstein Highway and Madrone Avenue, drew busloads of flower lovers on tours during the blooming season. Dolinsek also served on the Cotati City Council. The greenhouse site is now a mini-storage facility.

In the 1950s, Cotati had many active youth groups: Boy Scouts and Cub Scouts, Camp Fire Girls and Bluebirds, and a 4-H Club. At Christmas, Sophie Gwerder, who had bought the Cotati Inn and re-named it Sophie's, entertained all the children, and Santa produced gifts. Sophie Gwerder is pictured standing at rear next to Santa. (Courtesy of Marguerite Revard.)

A fashion show in 1954 was a big event for members of the Women's Improvement Club. Pictured, from left to right, are (front row) Mrs. J. Dunn, Jeanie Baker, Shirley O'Brien, Florence Chadwick, and Lois Boerstler; (back row) Dorothy Offutt, Claire Keyt, Mrs. William O'Brien, Helen Turney, Marie Ferrero, and Mrs. J. McDonald.

The Assembly of God Church began in Cotati in 1942, meeting first in rented quarters. In 1951 members started work on this church on East Cotati Avenue, and began holding services here in 1955. The church is still active.

Cotati Parent Nursery School opened in 1953 in a bungalow at the Cotati Motel. Since 1963 it has been in its present location on West Sierra Avenue at Henry Street. Pictured here in 1956, from left to right, are Eddie and Marsha Mendelssohn and an unidentified pupil at a school art show. The school is now known as the Cotati-Rohnert Park Cooperative Nursery School. (Courtesy of Cotati-Rohnert Park Cooperative Nursery School.)

As Cotati grew and Rohnert Park developed, a new and much expanded St. Joseph's Catholic Church was needed. A hilltop site on West Cotati Avenue adjacent to the new 101 Freeway was chosen in 1961, where the old Page Ranch barn had stood. The church was 197 feet long, 115 feet wide, and 97 feet high, with dramatic upswept beams and a skylight at the top. The church was dedicated on September 23, 1962 and is still in active use.

Cotati had been marshy since the days of the Coast Miwok Indians, and floods downtown were still frequent in the 1950s before Cotati Creek was improved. This photo shows Elmer Chadwick in his service station at the corner of what is now Old Redwood Highway and Henry Street about 1953. The building now houses Hines Signs.

W. Ray Miller and his family came to Cotati in 1955 when he became the first superintendent of the Cotati School District. He oversaw the rapid growth of the district when Rohnert Park began. Non-stop school construction, double sessions, and a school bus system were needed. He was also a Cotati city councilman, and active in many service organizations. He died while still in office in 1966. (Courtesy of Eleanor Miller.)

In the early 1950s mothers decided that Cotati School needed a kindergarten, so they set out to get one. They petitioned the school board, raised money for furniture and a play area, and moved the former school library to provide this room. Among the mothers pictured here celebrating their success, are Gerry Lipton, Dorothy Groom, Fern Jensen, Mary Sisk, Verna Shaw, Estelle Companey, Virginia Bruce, Hallene Cowan, Marguerite Revard, Ellie Wodrich, Annie Minatta, Mae Woodson.

Six

A NEW COLLEGE,
A NEW CITY,
A NEW AGE

In the late 1950s the California legislature announced plans for several new state colleges, including one in the area north of San Francisco. This set off an intense effort by several communities to obtain the college for their areas. Cotati was among them and, the Cotati Chamber of Commerce, led by Dr. Bill Kortum, lobbied all the other cities in Sonoma County to support the Cotati site. This float in a Petaluma parade in 1959 helped publicize the effort.

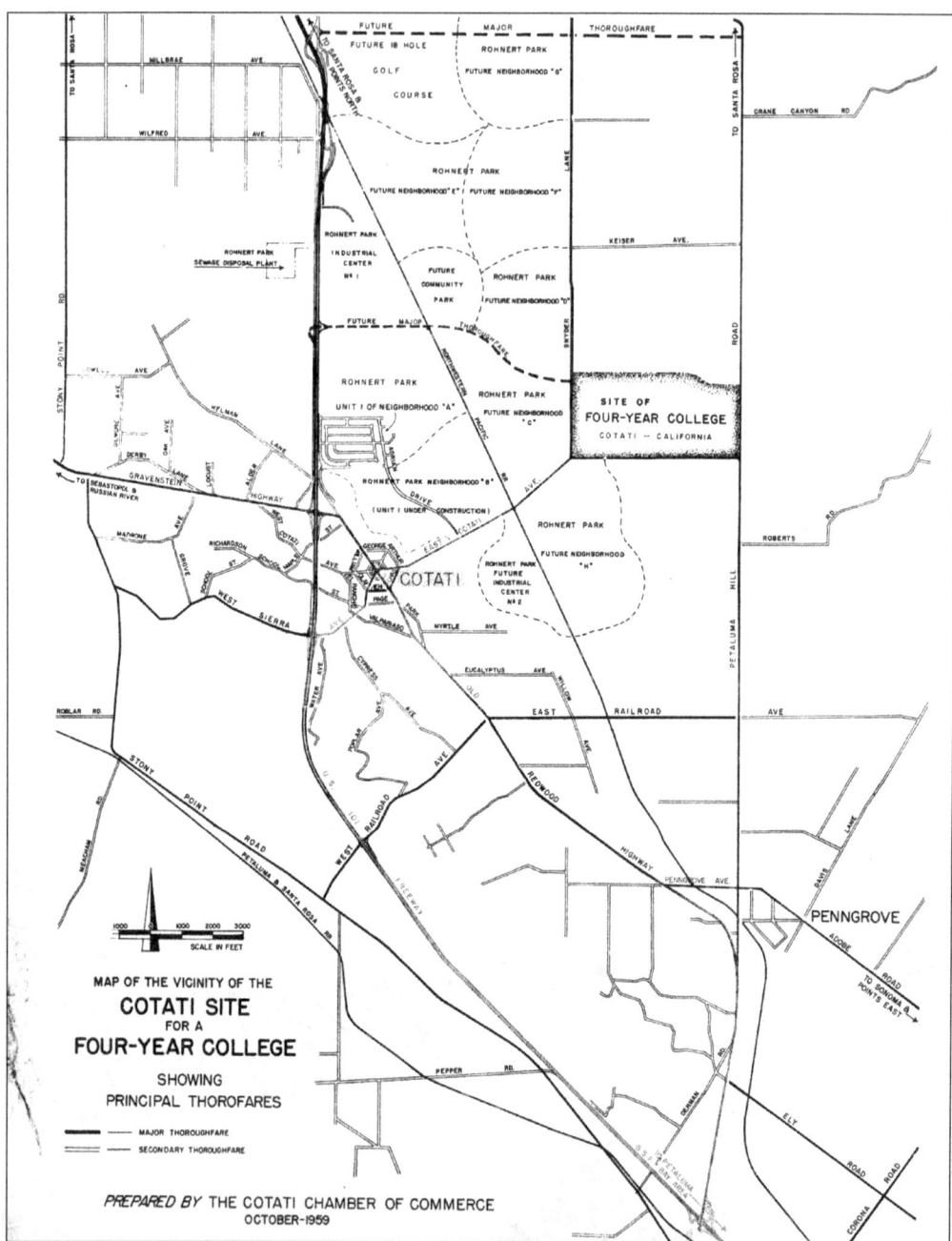

Flyers like the one pictured here were distributed in 1959 to help convince the State of California to select the former Forrest Benson ranch on East Cotati Avenue at Petaluma Hill Road as the site for a new state college in the North Bay Area. In the last minutes of the 1960 legislature, a bill authored by Senator Joseph Rattigan was passed authorizing the creation of Sonoma State College.

Sonoma State College's first president was Dr. Ambrose "Amby" Nichols, who had been a chemistry professor at San Diego State College. He had also taught radar during World War II, and was involved in the development of the atomic bomb, first at UC Berkeley and later at Oak Ridge, Tennessee. He was appointed president of the new college, which was not yet built, in 1961. He managed the first faculty in temporary buildings in Rohnert Park, and oversaw construction of the new campus. He stepped down as president in 1970, but continued on as a chemistry professor until 1976. A classroom building on the Sonoma State University campus is named for him, and in 1983 trustees of the state university system named him president emeritus. (Courtesy of Sonoma State University Archives.)

Bumper strips like this were distributed far and wide to help build support for the state college site on East Cotati Avenue. The natural rural beauty of the locale at the foot of the Sonoma Mountains was a selling point, as well as the central location in Sonoma County. When state college trustees arrived by bus to inspect the site, a Cotati Chamber of Commerce delegation greeted them with crates of crisp apples.

Soon after Sonoma State College opened, a group of local investors built Jack London Hall on East Cotati Avenue to serve as a student dormitory. Students did not find dormitory life particularly appealing, and it was not very successful venture. It is no longer standing. (Courtesy of Sonoma State University Archives.)

Sonoma State became a four-year university in 1978. The school's 25th anniversary was celebrated in 1985 with this Founder's Day gathering. Pictured, from left to right, are (front row) Lucy Kortum, Prue Draper, Eloise Oretsky, Betty Fredericks, and Jill Golis; (middle row) Don Leiffer, Leo Trepp, John Richardson, Maurice Fredericks, Tom Cox, Peter Golis, and Eugene Shepherd; (back row) David Benson (president), Ben Oretsky, Joseph Rattigan, Lloyd Draper, Bill Kortum, and Ambrose Nichols (president emeritus). (Courtesy of Sonoma State University Archives.)

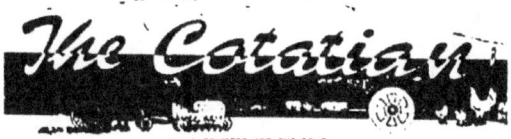

Welcome to Cotati; California's Newest City

The Cotatian
SW5 4014

The Cotatian, established in 1941 is published in Cotati, California where the famed 101 Highway is joined by the Gravenstein Highway which travels west through a famous apple country to the Russian River resort area and then to the Pacific Ocean.

ENLIGHTENMENT AND THE TRUTH

VOLUME 19   COTATI (Sonoma County) CALIFORNIA Thursday, July 1, 19.. $2 A Year   5c A Copy   NUMBER 30

CITY OF COTATI; 84% YES VOTE WINS

"On The Square" Houser, Chadwick, Olsson, Groom, Falletti Elected City Councilmen

LOOK TO THE FUTURE. COUNTY FAIR THEME

Cotati Firemen Rush To Rohnert Auto Crash

HUGE CROWD AT ELECTION

Startling news came to Cotati in 1955: Paul Golis and Maurice Fredericks were planning a new community on 2,600 acres of what had been the Waldo Rohnert Seed Company farmland just north of Cotati. The development progressed, the new community incorporated as the City of Rohnert Park, and many Cotatians saw their rural lifestyle threatened. A drive to incorporate Cotati succeeded, and on July 2, 1963, Cotati became a city. An effort had been made to extend the city limits out East Cotati Avenue to include the new college site, but that was not allowed by the state.

Sam Houser (*left*) was a county tax appraiser and a well-known Cotati citizen. He built support for the drive for incorporation, ran for the first city council, and was elected Cotati's first mayor.
Alfred Falletti (*right*) had been a director and president of the Cotati Public Utility District before the city was incorporated. He was elected to the new city's first council, and served terms as mayor in 1970–1971 and 1978–1979.

Cotati, "California's Newest City," celebrated its cityhood with a parade float of course. It is pictured here going through Petaluma in 1964.

In the early 1960s the Cotati post office served Rohnert Park and part of Penngrove, as well as Cotati. Henry Johnstone (center) was postmaster, Doris Vesgaard (left) was clerk, and Ralph Doyel (right) was the rural carrier.

John Curtis, a former California Highway Patrol officer, was Cotati's first chief of police. His trained dog, Birko, assisted him. Before incorporation, Cotati was served by the Sonoma County Sheriff's Office.

Early city council meetings were held in the firehouse. At this session Boy Scouts took honorary council seats. Pictured, from left to right, are unidentified, Rick Roberts, Terry Dillon, Councilman Stan Olsson, John Sklavos, unidentified, Mayor Lloyd Draper, unidentified Scout, Keith Wooley, Hank Wooley, and Birko (front). Cotati had incorporated on a tight budget, and had no permanent office or meeting place until 1971, when the school district abandoned Cotati Elementary School's old building and it became available at low cost to the city.

Students at Sonoma State loved the rural lifestyle in Cotati, and abandoned chickenhouses were quickly converted into apartments. Students brought new influences to the community.

Earth Day was first celebrated in San Francisco on March 21, 1970, and the concept immediately appealed to environmentally concerned young Cotatians. This huge papier-mâché ball was used in Cotati Earth Day celebrations during the 1970s and 1980s.

A gas station that had served the motoring public since Cotati's early automotive days became a popular bar and pool parlor. It was located south of town on Old Redwood Highway, where the Hunter's Ridge neighborhood is now. (Courtesy of Sonoma State University Archives.)

The Tradewinds tavern, in the north end of what had been the old Cotati Inn on Old Redwood Highway was a favorite haunt of the growing student population. It was here that the student drive began that unseated three old-timers on the city council in 1972, and here that two of the young councilmembers hatched a plan for stealing marijuana from the city's police evidence locker that led to their resignation in 1974. Tradewinds was established in 1965 by the late Jerry Green. In 1972 this sign was taken down to meet city sign regulations. In 1983 the business moved across the street to the location where it still operates. (Courtesy of Anthony Tusler.)

Student businesses began to develop in downtown Cotati. In 1968 what had been a general merchandise store on Old Redwood Highway became Cotati Company No. 2, run by students Liza and Brad Loop. They had a long corridor down the center, and on each side, rented spaces to student entrepreneurs. It had a bookstore, head shop, incense, candles, smoking paraphernalia, posters, and a restaurant. There were racks of free clothes, and a basket for spare change. Those who had it dropped it in; those who needed it were free to help themselves. This photo shows the business after it was gutted by fire in 1970. It has gone through several other identities, and is now the Redwood Cafe. (Courtesy of Anthony Tusler.)

Windmill Nursery was established in 1975 in a former home on LaPlaza, and operated successfully for many years. It later moved to the Gravenstein Intersection, and is still in business. (Courtesy of City of Cotati Planning Department.)

The influx of students and new neighborhoods led developer Hugh Codding to build the Rancho Cotate Center in the 500 block of East Cotati Avenue in 1973. It had a Farmer's Market, Cotati's first supermarket, and an assortment of other businesses including Rosie's Mexican Cantina, Persimmon Tree Cafe, Teddy Bear Sandwich Shop, Eye of the Rainbow health foods and tie-dyed t-shirts, a Western Auto Store, Eeyore's Book Store, Cougar's Den Barber Shop, Launderette, and a twin-theater movie house. Oliver's Market is now the major occupant of the center, with a large variety of smaller businesses. (Courtesy of City of Cotati Planning Department.)

Crocker Bank was another major tenant in the Rancho Cotate Center and the Cotati Post Office was moved here from its former site at the corner of Old Redwood Highway and William Street. Crocker Bank is no longer there and the building is now Video Droid. (Courtesy of City of Cotati Planning Department.)

Johnnie Frances Morgan helped bridge the gap between the students and the older generation. She worked in the 1970s with Kairos, a human services agency for young people on Old Redwood Highway, and from 1980 to 1986 managed a senior citizens' center called Second Beginning, which served low-cost meals.

Kotate Park opened in 1975 in the Holiday Park neighborhood of Cotati. City Councilwomen Tamara Davis (left) and Eve O'Rourke are pictured celebrating Earth Day.

This building on Old Redwood Highway was fashioned out of two old buildings from a lumber yard near the railroad tracks in the1930s. It had been a bakery, barber shop, and beauty shop in the 1940s and 1950s, and later became a craft shop. Pictured here in 1975, it had new tenants and arty signs more attuned to the growing student population. The building is still standing, and houses Nagomi Japanese Restaurant, A Cut Above hair salon, and Javatown coffee shop. (Courtesy of Anthony Tusler.)

Charlie Lorber, pictured in his Aquarius Pottery shop in 1975, was one of the new breed of business owners who set up shop in Cotati in the 1960s. He sold handmade clay artistry and taught classes in beginning pottery, presumably clothed. His shop was in the old Cotati Theater, which is now Finer Perceptions Used Book Shop. (Courtesy of Anthony Tusler.)

The business that came to typify Cotati in the minds of thousands of people was the Inn of the Beginning, launched in the former Cotati Inn building on Old Redwood Highway by Greg Cochrane and David McNair in 1968. It was dedicated to live music, and several musicians who achieved international fame got their start here. Cochrane later sold it to Ward Maillard, and Mark Braunstein later became a partner. The Grateful Dead, Arlo Guthrie, Waylon Jennings, and Jerry Garcia were among the artists who drew overflow crowds. The inn had several reincarnations, including a move to the old Women's Clubhouse as Cotati Cabaret. It finally closed in 2001, and the building houses Sweet Lou's jazz restaurant, Fran the Sandalady, and Spancky's. (Courtesy of Anthony Tusler.)

Flyers for the Inn of the Beginning were artwork in themselves, produced by Fran Fleet, a woodcarver and leather worker who had a small shop in the building called Trespassers W. She had been one of the youthful shopkeepers in Cotati Company No. 2, and carved the artistic redwood sign for the Inn of the Beginning and Tradewinds. (Courtesy of Steve Jones.)

for the finest *Live Music*
in the North Bay Area

March 81

SUN 1 Mission Mt. Wood Band $4.50

WED 4 ORDER NEW SANDALS — THE SANDALADY
8201a OLD REDWOOD HWY
COTATI, CALIFORNIA

THU 5 BORN READY / THE EDGE $3

FRI 6 Greg Kihn Band THE TITANS
8pm and 10:30 pm $6

SAT 7 Roseanne Cash and the CHERRY BOMBS
8pm and 10:30 pm $6

SUN 8 "TURNTABLE TIME" with RASTA LOUIE
8pm $1.50

MON 9 DAVE BRADY OCTET $2.50

WED 18 BETSY LUCAS BAND / the CHILLS $1

THU 19 Mel Martin Quartet $3.50

FRI 20 Tazmanian Devils and THE EDGE $4.50

SAT 21 The Impostors and THE DEFECTORS $3.50

SUN 22 NEW DEAL RHYTHM BAND $3.50

WED 11 John Fahey / GEORGE WINSTON
8pm and 10:30 pm $5

THU 12 Kate Wolf and Nina Gerber $4

FRI 13 MERLIN $4

SAT 14 THE RUBINOOS
THE TITANS $3.50

SUN 15

MON 16 THE SONOMA JAZZ ORCHESTRA $2.50

TUE 24 "TURNTABLE TIME" / RASTA LOUIE
8pm $1.50

WED 25 PICK UP NEW SANDALS — THE SANDALADY
8201a OLD REDWOOD HWY
COTATI, CALIFORNIA

THU 26 BIG WHEELS $2.50

FRI 27 Queen Ida / BON TON ZYDECO BAND
PETER ALSOP $4

SAT 28 Back in the Saddle $4.50

SUN 29

This flyer from March 1981 features the late folksinger Kate Wolf, who went on to wide fame after her gigs at the Inn of the Beginning. Roseanne Cash, after starting with her father, Johnny Cash, played the Inn as guitarist with a band called the Cherry Bombs. (Courtesy of Steve Jones.)

Cotati's population was growing rapidly in the 1970s, when Windmill Farms was built adjacent to East Cotati Avenue. Louise Santero and her husband, Angelo (Shorty), were avid gardeners, and still cultivated part of the old family ranch in the shadow of encroaching homes. (Courtesy of Donna Stegman.)

A favorite new business was the Brass Ass Saloon on East Cotati Avenue. Another branch of the Brass Ass was in Santa Rosa, and they inspired one of Cotati's most popular festivals, the Ass to Ass Race, which each summer from 1982 to 1986 challenged runners and walkers to race from one Brass Ass to the other, ending with a musical party in the Cotati Plaza. Pictured modeling shirts from the race are members of the authors' family, from left to right, Shirley Black, Erin Draper, Bob Draper, and Robin Draper.

Seven

Cotati Encounters the Counter Culture

Cotati Freestore was a street theater group that performed in Cotati and anywhere else they found a welcome. They were frequently seen in San Francisco's Union Square and on the UC Berkeley campus. Pictured here, from left to right, are (front row) Sue Paulekas, Phreekus Paulekas, Vito Paulekas, Tamara, and Karl Franconi. Also shown are Steven Snake, Sky Paulekas, Glen Sakko, Peggy Farmer, Yanna, Lorene Allen, Ricky Applebaum, and Michael Wednesday. (Courtesy of B.B. Paulekas.)

Vito Paulekas, pictured here *c.* 1975, was the heart and soul of the New Wave in Cotati. A talented artist and sculptor, musician and dancer, he had gained fame in Southern California and in the San Francisco Bay Area. He and his wife, Sue, came to Cotati in 1969, and he was the mentor and inspiration for many of the creative young people in town. Vito died in 1992 but some of his family members still live in Cotati. (Courtesy of B.B. Paulekas.)

Vito took the name of his street theater group from the Cotati Free Store, a shack in the Plaza where people could leave clothing to be picked up by others who needed them. The result was an eclectic appearance for the wearers that became known as "the Cotati Look." The group is pictured here in 1973 on Old Redwood Highway. (Courtesy of B.B. Paulekas.)

Life wasn't all mellow however. In that era of the SLA (Symbionese Liberation Army) and hostage-taking, Cotati Police Chief Tom Gray felt Cotati might be threatened, and organized a SWAT Squad. This photo on the front page in the *Cotati Call* newspaper on October 23, 1975, raised such an outcry that the team was disbanded. Pictured, left to right, are Rick Standish, Ed McLean, Jim Baker, Bob Morris, Blaine Kimball, and Jim Brown. (Courtesy of J. Pat Geis.)

Vito decided that the Cotati Plaza needed a bandstand, so he recruited helpers, salvaged lumber and built one about 1972. Performances by the Freestore troupe and anyone else who enjoyed making music were spontaneous and ongoing. (Courtesy of B.B. Paulekas.)

A stained-glass window made for the bandstand was typical of the new art forms that began appearing around Cotati.

The Cotati Co-op was one of the first health food stores, operated by a board of directors, with some volunteer workers, and it was much-loved by a large clientele. It was located in the former Cotati Realty Company building at the corner of Old Redwood Highway and Charles Street. The Co-op disbanded in 1994, and the store immediately became Tama-Rama's, still one of Cotati's popular eating and socializing spots. The handsome carved wooden sign is on display at the Redwood Cafe.

The Cotati Answering Service was one of several businesses that moved into what had been residences around the Plaza about 1974, and advertised itself with a distinctive sign.

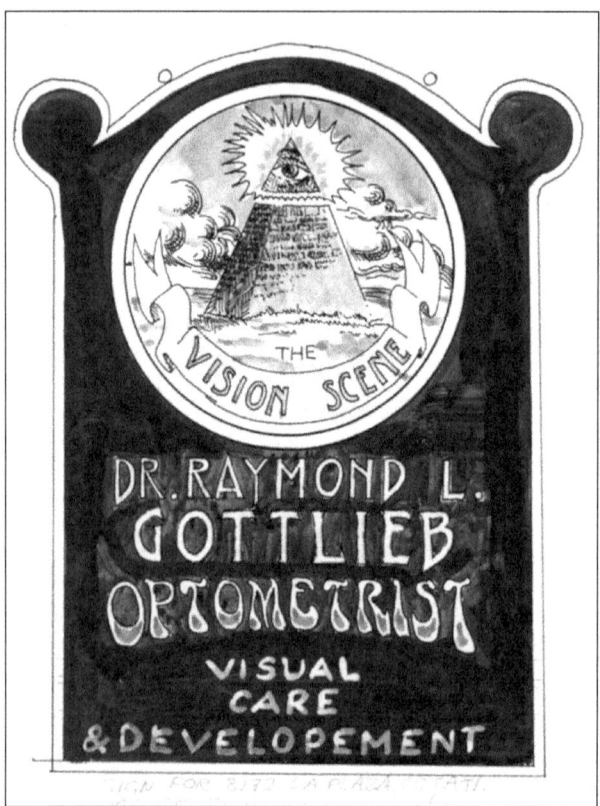

As sketches on these pages illustrate, new businesses that came to Cotati had unusually ornamental signs, and were even identified by a city councilwoman as public art. Some of their business offerings were dramatic too, this c. 1975 optometrist provided treatment that included focusing on an eye chart while jumping on a trampoline. His office was located in what had been a residence on LaPlaza. (Courtesy of City of Cotati Planning Department.)

This artistic sign was designed by Brian Elder in 1976 for a tavern in what had been the Wigwam Cafe, and previously the San Francisco Glass Company on Old Redwood Highway. The building now houses Zone Music and other businesses. (Courtesy of City of Cotati Planning Department.)

This popular eating establishment illustrated the eye-catching signs that had become typical of Cotati in the 1960s and 1970s. It was in the Inn of the Beginning building in 1972. (Courtesy of City of Cotati Planning Department.)

This sign with its multi-colored spaceship and silver letters adorned a garage/service station on Old Redwood Highway at Henry Street in the 1980s. Joel's Harmony Garage is still in business in the same building as Zone Music on Old Redwood Highway. (Courtesy of City of Cotati Planning Department.)

Vito Paulekas, a sculptor as well as a builder and performer, believed that Cotati should honor its Indian heritage and in 1980 he produced this 9-foot-tall statue of Chief Cotate in the Plaza. He explained that "Chief Cotate was dancing on the nipple of the breast of Mother Earth which gives life to all of us." The statue was constructed of cement composite and decorated with stained glass. It began disintegrating in later years. In 1993 Chief Cotate was renovated by a group of Indian artists, a mural added, and a protective shelter built over it. It is still a landmark in LaPlaza Park.

Radical student demonstrations in other parts of the country were seen in Cotati too. This one, in 1973 in front of the bandstand in the Plaza, followed a march by thousands of students from Sonoma State College. (Courtesy of Gary Isha Isringhaus.)

The 8-Ball, a downtown tavern that had been a popular gathering place for Cotati since the 1940s, and was the scene of an anti-nuclear demonstration about 1974. Pictured standing at right is Marlene Blankenship, wife of the owner, with an unidentified visitor and anonymous "victim." (Courtesy of Gary Isha Isringhaus.)

Several counter-culture newspapers were published in the 1970s and 1980s in Cotati, but none survived more than a few years. One was the *Bugle*, and the staff is pictured here at a last get-together in September 1973. Included here are (front row) Michael Funke and Anthony Tusler; (middle row) Beverly Carrillo, Mary Carrillo, Nancy Gunn, Martin Tusler, Marilyn Kinghorn, David Kinghorn, and Toni Novak; (back row) David MacPhail, Rob Weinstein, Chuck Idelson, Hans vonBoldrick, Mark Thiesen, Michael Martin, Brian Elder, Simon Agree, Steve Laughlin, Irv Sutley, Michael Stephens, and several unidentified members. (Courtesy of Anthony Tusler.)

LaPlaza Park in the 1970s became a place to gather with friends, to play drums and guitars, to dance, and to sleep with your dogs. (Courtesy of Gary Isha Isringhaus.)

The Last Great Hiding Place was a cafe, and at various times a movie house and performance theater in the center of the downtown. Employees and customers are pictured here. It is now the Redwood Café. (Courtesy of Redwood Café.)

After the demise of the Inn of the Beginning in 1982, manager Mark Braunstein and building owner Ken Frankel moved the business to the Women's Clubhouse, newly dubbed the Cotati Cabaret. It continued there featuring popular musicians until 1988, when it closed. (Courtesy of Sonoma State University Archives.)

A new group of imaginative Cotati citizens came to represent the town's mainstream population. Mr. Fine, pictured here in 1973, was one of the best known. He drove a purple Cadillac painted with the slogan, "Have Love, Will Travel" and was known for his ornate cane and greeting of "My cousin-brother!" that was always accompanied by a large hug and often a kiss on the cheek. (Courtesy of Anthony Tusler.)

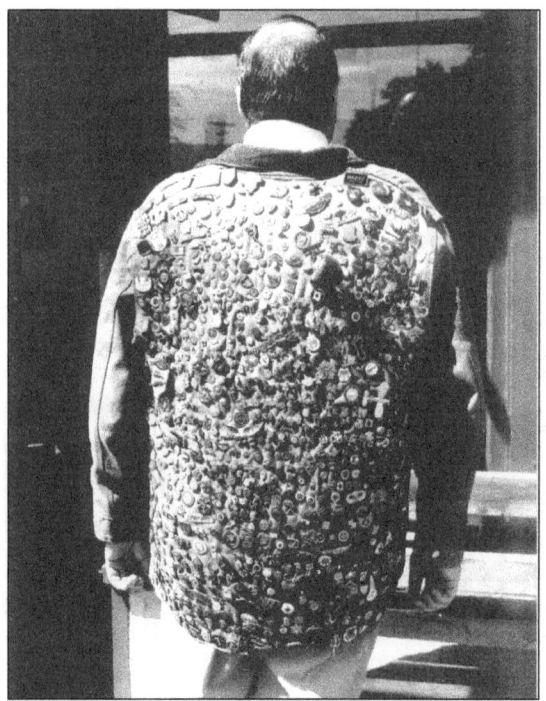

David Roth, pictured at left, was seen around town everywhere, and came to be called "Mr. Cotati." He covered the town on his bicycle every day, and knew almost everyone he encountered. He was proud of the coat he is pictured wearing about 1975, covered with publicity badges, campaign buttons, and souvenirs. (Courtesy of Gary Isha Isringhaus.)

In the 1940s, 1950s, and 1960s, Sophus Jensen's blacksmith shop on LaPlaza was the place where old-timers gathered to share news, get repair jobs done, or sip from the jug of red wine that always sat in the corner. Jensen, pictured here about 1952, had been in business in Cotati since the early 1920s.

The Jensen blacksmith shop became the Barrel of Suds in the 1970s, and people still met there to swap stories. Pictured here are members of the Bronze Hog, a favorite local band, from left to right, Richard Hughes, Ed Farmer, Don Connally, Frank Hayhurst, and Michael McCarthy. The building is now Dos Amigos Mexican Restaurant. (Courtesy of Anthony Tusler.)

In the late 1980s and 1990 Cotati honored its heritage with an Indian Summer Festival that drew hundreds to the Plaza to watch dances and share Native American foods. (Courtesy of Gary Isha Isringhaus.)

Eight

AN INTERESTING, IF RELUCTANT, BLEND

A newspaper reporter in 1975 described Cotati as "an interesting if reluctant blend of the old and the new, conservative and radical." Michael Larrain is one of the young businessmen who came to Cotati in the counter culture years and used his imagination—and a little help from Tennyson—to appeal to both elements of the community. He has sold flowers from his car on East Cotati Avenue for over 30 years, in summer and winter, rain or shine, a permanent part of the colorful Cotati scene.

Fran Fleet, a young artisan/entrepreneur, came to Cotati and started her business in the Cotati Company No. 2 in the 1960s, as a wood carver, candlemaker, and sandalmaker. She carved many of the artistic signs that identified Cotati businesses, moved her shop, Trespassers W, to the Inn of the Beginning building, and designed the Inn's dramatic flyers. As the years went by, she began to specialize in repairing and reconditioning baseball gloves, and now, as Fran The Sandalady, has a national reputation, her own website, and more gloves to work on than she can count.

Jim Boggio was one of the founders of the Cotati Accordion Festival in the LaPlaza Park in 1991, along with Rebecca Brown, Clifton Buck-Kaufman, and several others. It became tremendously successful, and when Boggio died suddenly in 1996, friends and accordion aficionados decided to remember him with a larger-than-life-size bronze statue in the center of the park. Blair Hardman, a longtime friend and fellow musician, led the effort, and the statue, sculpted by Jim Kelly, was unveiled at the Seventh Annual Accordion Festival in 1997. Friends always put a Santa hat on the statue at Christmas, and appropriate decorations on other holidays.

.50¢
Souvenir
Program

COTATI
ACCORDION
FESTIVAL

SAT. & SUN~AUG. 24,25,1991

This program for the first Accordion Festival was placid compared to some that have followed in the ensuing years—one year it was a gorilla, one year Mona Lisa; others had Albert Einstein and assorted far-out characters, all playing accordions. The event, now in its 13th year, draws thousands to Cotati to enjoy the rollicking melodies, dance the polka in tents, and play or listen to non-stop multi-cultural accordion music. Proceeds benefit several Cotati educational institutions.

11th annual

cotati
jazz
festival
June 15-16, 1991

Music of all kinds has been important in Cotati ever since the days of the old Men of Melody band in the early 1900s. Since 1980 the city has staged a jazz festival with well-known artists playing in several of the city's restaurants, taverns, and shops. Since 1999, summer classical music concerts have been produced by the Cotati Philharmonic Orchestra, in LaPlaza Park and in other venues in the winter. (Courtesy of Jud Snyder.)

A musical center for serious musicians and recording artists is located in this building on Old Redwood Highway near Gravenstein Intersection. Zone Music and Recording, Backstage Technical Service, and World Class Guitar Amplifiers are among the businesses now in the building that was constructed in 1951 by William Appleton for his San Francisco Glass Company.

This building at the 101-Gravenstein Intersection was built in the 1940s by Floyd Winter for his Sonoma Mattress factory and furniture store. He and his son Herb Winter and their families operated the business for over 40 years. The Sea Horse Tavern was in one section in 1979 when this photo was taken The building has been extensively remodeled and is now home to Back Door Records and Tapes, Windmill Nursery, Mike's Hamburgers, and several other businesses. (Courtesy of John Hughes.)

Cotati's past—and a bit of the future as well—are illustrated by these buildings on LaPlaza, where the old Robert Ross General Store and the Cotati Hotel once stood. The small building, a treasured relic, is the Schuman Brothers Shoe Repair Shop. Directly next to it is the brand new mixed-use retail and apartment residential building built by Anna Young and opened in the spring of 2003.

Past Cotati mayors looked to the future at the city's 30th anniversary in 1993. Pictured, from left to right, are (front row) Stanley Olsson, Bill Miller, Katherine Roberts, Jim Wirt, Linda Shorey, Bob Davis, Alan Stansbury, Harry Fassio, and Al Falletti; (back row) Richard Cullinan, Sandy Ellis, Harold Berkemeier, and Eve O'Rourke.

An aerial view of Cotati's distinctive hexagonal downtown is centered by LaPlaza Park. It is, in all ways, the heart of the city, site of many memorial structures, bandstand, play area, and picnic facilities. It has been the scene of festive gatherings since the town's earliest days.

CPSIA information can be obtained
at www.ICGtesting.com
Printed in the USA
BVHW010941101118
532427BV00027B/761/P